# The Conflict Between the Individual and Society in the Plays of JAMES BRIDIE

*By*
*ERNEST G. MARDON, Ph.D.*
*University of Lethbridge*

WILLIAM MACLELLAN

Embryo Books are published by
William MacLellan
17 Woodside Place, Glasgow, C.3.

Printed by James Bell & Sons, Hamilton.

**THE CONFLICT
BETWEEN THE
INDIVIDUAL &
SOCIETY IN TH
PLAYS OF
JAMES BRIDIE**

QUEEN MARGARET COLLEGE

LIBRARY

Please return book on or before latest date
stamped below

# CONTENTS

*Dedication*

*TO*

*MA Y*

*"Again and again and
again and again we have
covered
the face of the earth with order
and loveliness
and a little justice.
But only the face of it.
Deep down below the subterranean brutes
have bided their time
to shake down our churches
and palaces
and let loose the little rats to sport
among the ruins."*

DAPHNE LAUREOLA

# CHAPTER I

## INTRODUCTION

The twentieth century, called the 'Age of Anxiety', is one in which the traditional beliefs and values have disappeared, leaving an unfilled gap in the lives of men. Developments in science and medicine have resulted in our knowing much more about "what we are", but they have failed to tell us, "who we are". In this age of disinte - grating values, James Bridie, the Scottish dramatist, is primarily concerned with portraying individuals who deviate from the norm of acceptable patterns of behaviour. All through his writing career, he was interested in the problems facing persons who must adjust to the demands of society while feeling a strong urge to retain their individuality. Bridie mainly wrote plays in which such harsh realities as death, crime, mental disease and drunkenness are accepted as part of human existence.

Bridie, who was born Osborne Hunry Mavor on January 3, 1888, in Glasgow, Scotland, became a physician on the urging of his father. He obtained wide experience as a doctor in his native city and in the Royal Army Medical Corps during the Great War. He did not turn to writing until he was forty. Due to his important position as a Glasgow medical specialist, he used a 'nom-de-plume'. He obtained his pseudonym of James Bridie by combining his grandfather's Christian name with his grandmother's maiden name.

In his dramas, Bridie discusses the eternal problems facing man in our strongly conformist society. His experiences as a doctor and his medical training mean that he understands the various mental ailments that affect mankind. His protagonists suffer from mental disorders which he examines in a clinical-like fashion on the stage.

In this work, it will be shown that James Bridie's major concern and preoccupation is in portraying characters who rebel in one form or another against mass conformity, which is one of the marks of contemporary society. He has no use for the individual who does not remain true to his inner self. He, however, does not give any solutions to the vexing problems facing us.

Besides sympathizing with the rebel, Bridie does much subtle questioning of normally accepted values. He never takes anything for granted, or merely at its face value. He worries about good and evil. His probing uneasy mind is forever attempting to get behind the surface. He appears to detest those who think they know everything and have some easy solution to the problems of human existence. [1]

His dramas have not only a highly cultivated and sophisticated wit, and an intellectual restlessness, but also considerable depth. Bridie's plays are all modern in spirit, even when based on Scottish medical crime reports of the early nineteenth century or Old Testament subjects. They are concerned with problems of contemporary life and our modern urban civilisation. For his protagonists, as we shall see, truth has as many faces as a nightmare; and one is left with the impression that each individual must create his own set of standards.

The detrimental effects of social, national and racial tensions, resentment and prejudice are, of course, among the commonest themes in twentieth century literature. But Bridie is a member of the small group of contemporary dramatists, who, in their work, display a vital realistic awareness of such tensions and prejudices. The result of this awareness is that Bridie's leading characters, even though they may be mentally unbalances, are treated by him in an understanding and sympathetic manner.

Bridie was not chiefly concerned in propounding any philosophy, but with the careful examination and clinical study of a few selected individual characters. He shows his skill as a playwright by the manner in which he combines extreme contrasts within the often mentally unstable characters that he portrays on the stage. Bridie was not interested in using the theatre to expound his personal views, or any political theories. He is primarily interested in learning, if possible, why men act as they do. He was fascinated by the enigma of man and of life. As one of his characters says:

Who knows the heart of a man, and what moves in the darkness?

In studying the plays of James Bridie, it is important to realize that he is not a 'closet dramatist'. In order fully to understand his plays, one should see them on the stage. Tennessee Williams put this need to see a play acted in the theatre thus:

In my opinion, a play in a book is

only the shadow of a play and not even a clear shadow of it.....The printed script of a play is hardly more than an architect's blueprint of a house not yet built, or built and destroyed. The colour, the grace and levitation, the structural pattern in motion, the quick interplay of live beings, suspended like fitful lightning c l o u d s, these things are the play, not the words on paper, nor thoughts and ideas of an author, t h o s e  s h a b b y things snatched off basement counters at Gimbel's.[3]

Frequently, critics in their discussion of Bridie's plays appear to have totally forgotten this.

Even though Bridie was a gifted prose-writer, he did not write much about his own critical theories of drama. He did, however, say that a play is not a play until it is performed in front of an audience.[4] In the same article, he defines what he understands the institution of the theatre to mean:

A play is a method of passing an interval of time. A stage play is a method of passing an interval of time by putting an actor or actors on a platform and causing them to say or do certain things. If it is amusing, that is to say it succeeds in making

the spectators unconscious of the
passage of time, it fulfills its function
and has merit. If, on the other hand,
the spectators are conscious of the
passage towards destruction and
nothingness, the play has failed and
has no merit, or, at least, no merit
as a play. Other qualities of a play
— its education, its thought-provoking,
its exciting, its poetic qualities — are
not basic.[5]

Here, Bridie makes it quite plain that he
feels the first and primary function of a
play is to entertain the audience. He
goes on to explain his views:

The theatre is a Pass-time.....the
eternal function of the theatre is to
entertain, to suspend, or at least,
make tolerable the business of living.
To produce belief is the principle
trick in this particular device of
passing time. In passing let me tell
you that passing Time is no mean or
frivolous activity. The consciousness of Time is a very terrible thing
.....A play makes us believe that
we are taking part in a fuller kind of
life that that in which we live with its
long, unbearably flat passages and
longueurs. These longueurs are
absent in dreams, and to induce a sort
of dream state is part of the trick.[6]

We have to judge Bridie's plays in the light of his stated aims, and not as examples of dramas written with the various, often conflicting so-called 'rules' in mind. We know that Bridie did not follow the accepted dramatic techniques and dramatic devices laid down by experts when he wrote his plays. His was an original genius; he offers no solutions nor do his characters, who seldom live happily ever after.

It is a recognised fact that Bridie did not get along well with the drama critics who reviewed his plays when they first appeared on the stage. The literary critics have in many cases merely parroted the statements of the original misconceptions about Bridie's aims and methods of dramatic composition.

J.B. Priestley, who was a successful playwright at the same time as Bridie, remarks that he was a defiant, wilful, impudent, brilliant amateur who became the victim of his own 'persona'. The drama critics were deceived into finding what Bridie only pretended to be and seldom discovered what he was trying to do. [7]

We feel that Priestley is c o m p l e t e l y wrong when he says Bridie, whose plays are standing up to the test of time, is an 'amateur'. It is true that Bridie did not attempt to become a merely popular dramatist, but he did try with a great deal of success to give a freshness and vigour to his plays that appeal first to the intellect and then to the emotions.

One of the most persistent criticisms of Bridie by his detractors is that he fails to write a good third act. In his autobiography, the author dismisses this charge in a lordly fashion:

> And all this nonsense about last acts. Only God can write last acts, and He seldom does. You should go out of the theatre with your head whirling with speculations. You should be lovingly selecting infinite possibilities for characters you have seen on the stage. What further interest for you have they, if they are neatly wrapped up and bedded or confined? It makes me angry to hear these doctrinaire duds. [8]

That Bridie was often misunderstood by his contemporary critics can be seen by referring to the old reviews in "The Spectator", "The New Statesman and Nation" and "Theatre Arts Monthly". They have attacked him as a craftsman, at times to the exclusion of any consideration of the themes being developed in his play and the possible appropriateness of the structure, however diffuse, to his theme.

For example, George Jean Nathan described Bridie as "a man of ideas and talents whose assembly line activity did not allow him to do justice to them".[9]

Nathan goes on to explain that he feels there is about most of Bridie's work an unmeditated air and slap-dash preparation that gives it the sense of a first draft. Shreds of the fantastic and whimsical mix awkwardly with patches of conventional polite comedy and the pseudo-philosophical, as for example, according to Nathan, in "Daphne Laureola". The recognisable and believable collide with the farfetched and silly.[10]

This critic fails to realize that Bridie obtains dramatic unity through the development of his characters who are finally abandoned in a confused and puzzling world. Nathan misses the point of Bridie's plays which are developed in a non-traditional manner.

The juxtaposition of opposites, of the conventional with the fantastic, the believable with the silly, is an integral part of Bridie's dramatic method which involves the use of contrasts. It is through the clever juxtaposition of opposites that the dramatist reveals the complexity of his characters, and develops his predominant concern for the ever present conflict between the individual and society.

G.S. Fraser in "The Modern Writer

and his World" maintains:

> Bridie never really learned how to
> construct a play: his three-act plays
> often resemble three brilliant first
> acts of three quite different ideal
> plays, none of which he has had the
> courage to push through to an end
> along a single line of development.
> But partly because of this very
> digressiveness, his 'language' is
> much more alive than Galsworthy's
> or indeed than Priestley's. [11]

However, Fraser does admit that Bridie,
as a playwright, with all his faults, is
superior to most of his contemporaries
who wrote for the British stage during
the 1930's and 1940's. It is curious that
he is not better known in North America.

Occasionally, a critic does attempt
to give a balanced assessment of James
Bridie as a dramatist, but more often a
misleading label, such as "The Scottish
Shaw", has been tacked on to him. Frederick Lumley believes that Bridie, with
his dry sense of humour and his philosophical wit, saved the London stage from
stagnation during the twenty years of his
dramatic career. [12]

Another critic who has been quick to
recognise Bridie's worth is William
Jeffrey, who observed:

His influence in the theatre has been
salutary. When it seemed as if modern comedy was about to commit
'Hari-Kari' by reducing speech to a
minimum, along came Bridie with a
train of characters everyone of whom
will talk twenty to the dozen and leave
the welkin. All in all, Bridie has
devised plays rich in entertainment
and generous in the number of good
parts for players. [13]

However, one cannot have preconceived
ideas of dramatic form in order to
appreciate Bridie's plays. One must be
willing to look at the plays themselves
to see what they are. Inconclusiveness,
or ambiguity, is inherent in the very
structure of a Bridie play because the
plays are arguments in which the balance
of thesis and antithesis is maintained.
The conclusion is never a resolution because basic to the underlying structure
of his dramas are arguments about, or
searches for, truth.

Eric Linklater, a personal friend of
Bridie for years, throws light on the
dramatist's love for arguments:

It is, I believe, Bridie's conception
of drama-as-argument that has led
to a loose-thinking but common complaint against him. [14]

The complaint is that Bridie loses interest in the conclusion of his dramas, ending them before his story is ended. Linklater declares:

> This complaint comes from critics who, because they are looking for a purely dramatic 'denouement', have lost sight of the argument. The play finishes when the argument is finished. [15]

That Bridie conceived of drama as argument, that he believed in and demonstrated the theatrical value of discussion seems clear. Linklater explained his views of the value of discussion thus:

> It is a common matter of observation that when two men in a railway carriage begin to discuss any general topic the other occupants put down the most enthralling of books and newspapers and listen. In the theatre today, if two duellists were to put down their rapiers and daggers to elaborate a casual remark by one of them about, say, the eradication of musk-rats, be assured that the audience would lean forward in its seats and listen with breathless attention. [16]

This is exactly what Bridie does in many of his plays, and, we note, the conclusion of the argument is never a resolution of the drama in the traditional sense of the word. One of the playwright's Scottish friends, Moray McLaren, explains that a play is a 'flow of the soul' rather than a 'feast of the reason'.[17] McLaren adds that, to the Irish and the Scots, an argument that reaches a conclusion has failed. It is plain that the critic who is looking for a nicely rounded out play, with all the loose ends tied up, will have to go to another dramatist. Bridie never wrote a well-made play. As we will see, he developed his own dramatic methods, and never conformed to the accepted mode of play-writing.

The fact that Bridie was a sincere agnostic may have influenced his choice of material. He rebelled, like many of his characters, against the Calvanistic environment in which he was raised. But he always remained vitally concerned with ethical problems facing modern man, especially the physician. Bridie, moreover, knew his moral idiom and delighted in theological speculation.

His characters like to argue especially about momentous subjects which they 'thoroughly understand' or merely for the sake of argument. As has been observed, Bridie was concerned with the struggle between good and evil in society.

This issue exercises Bridie's mind most strenuously and calls forth his best work. However, there is nothing sententious or evangelical about Bridie's approach. This is one of the marked differences between him and many of his contemporaries. Indeed, Bridie's best plays are not obviously religious plays at all despite the fact that, at first glance, some of his titles would convey the opposite impression.[18]

On the whole, the plays of Bridie present an optimistic point of view of life. He is a tolerant moralist. Unlike Priestley, he is little concerned with social propaganda. Bridie, who was an acute observer of man, shows a shrewd sense of character throughout his work, a sense developed, no doubt, by the experience he gained when he was a medical practitioner.[19] At any rate, he delights in poking fun at man's foibles without preaching. His characters are, without exception, interesting people, the good are never too good and the bad are always human. With his main protagonists, Bridie has a bond of sympathy and understanding.

It is worth noting that Peter Westland says Bridie probably excels any playwright living in the first half of this century, not excluding the greatest.[20]

His plays earn our respect even while they stir our emotions, or suitably move our sense of humour. However, Westland believes that Bridie was erratic in his choice of subjects, in the handling of his themes, and was occasionally obscure. Nevertheless, against these faults must be balanced his ability to make unusual scenes wholly convincing, his delicacy of characterization, and the sound structure of his plays based on the skilful use of contrasts. Westland concludes:

> Over and above Bridie's merits as a dramatist is the unmistakable illumination of his mind and burning zeal.[21]

A study of his work reveals that Bridie had tolerance, boundless enthusiasm, humanity and a healing good humour.

Allardyce Nicoll summed up Bridie thus:

> Gifted with an individual sense of humour and a magnificent command of theatrical prose, he commanded attention because of his versatility, his appreciation of character values and his fine dramatic sensitivity. Unfortunately, to these virtues he added a serious weakness: so active was his mind that constantly, as he was approaching the completion of a

particular play, his imagination went leaping ahead of its successor. [22]

Here, even Allardyce Nicoll fails to realize the real reason for the apparent formlessness of structure in Bridie's plays. The examination of the plays reveals that the criticism of Bridie's supposed formless structure is not valid. In fact, the opposite is the case. Bridie's approach and method are ideally suited to the depiction of the theme of conflict. The result of this is that his plays are much less dated than those of his contemporaries.

The dilema of modern man is the theme that runs through all of Bridie's major plays. In the six plays selected for careful examination in this work, the central conflict revolves around the inability of the protagonist to adjust to society. These plays are representative of the best of Bridie's forty works. However, the theme will be found to be dominant in many of his other plays. The principle of selection has been to take three of his early, pre-World War II, dramas and three plays from the postwar period. The plays deal with the adjustment of the individual to society. In the first group — "The Switchback" (1928) and "Mr. Gillie" (1950), the non-conformist protagonists are able to adjust to the disturbance of accepted standards of value. The second group — "The Last Trump" (1938) and "Daphne Laureola" (1949), deals with mentally ill characters who cut themselves off from living fruitful lives. The final group — "The Anatomist" (1930) and "Dr. Angelus" (1947), demonstrates protagonists who are mentally disturbed to such a degree that the protagonists attack society by committing murder in the case of Angelus, and by condoning murder in the case of Knox.

In these plays Bridie expresses a faith in and a fondness for the individual, a mistrust of institutions, such as government and the Church, a distaste for social compulsion, a suspicion of the over-dedicated man. He also expresses a feeling for a Creator who is distant and impersonal, unconcerned with and uninvolved in the activities of men.

We shall see that his plays become more pessimistic in tone as he grew older, and watched the world he had known as a young man change. He observed first hand the blighting effects of the two holocausts of this century, and lived on into the grim, grey austerity of socialistic Britain.

We shall investigate the types of

27

characters which Bridie creates to illustrate his major concern. We shall see
that his protagonists who follow the dictates of their own hearts, may be failures
in the eyes of the world, but at the same
time they feel that they have succeeded
by remaining true to their principles.
The mentally ill and criminal characters
are portrayed as finding it impossible to
come to terms with society, and to live
fruitful existences. Their failure is due
in part to the lack of recognizable objective values and standards of behaviour.

It will be shown that plays studied in
this work form a distinctive group of
dramas in which Bridie repeats his dominant theme of the quest of the individual
to adjust to his modern environment and
yet maintain his integrity. The dramatist
is showing us different kinds, not degrees,
of individualism in the six plays under
investigation. The kind of individualism
examined in "The Switchback" and "Mr.
Gillie" is based on inner integrity, and
the protagonists accept traditional sets
of values. They are not concerned by
society's rejection of them. In the fourth
chapter, the kind of individualism that
Bridie is probing involves the struggle
for identity of characters who do not have
any inner convictions. In the third group
of two plays, discussed in chapter five,

the dramatist shows us protagonists who have inner convictions, but who have twisted values and lack humanity. The first group deals with the nonconformist, the second with mentally ill persons and the third group with characters who attempt to undermine the social fabric of society. In each group, one play is taken from the early, pre-World War II works of Bridie, and one from the later, postwar plays. They indicate that Bridie's work became grimmer and more pessimistic in tone as he grew older.

It is proposed to examine the characters in each play and see how they develop and change during the course of the action. However, we must realize that the denouement of one of his dramas will not be the traditional unravelling of the plot. Bridie was primarily interested in framing questions, not in attempting to answer them. Nevertheless, his plays have dramatic unity and focus, if we realize that, for a Bridie character, a quest for identity is all important.

While pondering over the question of good and evil, right and wrong, Bridie appears at times to side with the social outcasts. The dramatic unity of his plays arises from the fact that the problems he discusses have no resolution in themselves. The absence of resolution forms an integral part of the meaning of the drama and is what actually culminates the thematic structure. He shows his characters facing real-life decisions, the kind of decisions which each man must work out himself. His protagonists are often unable to resolve such conflicts with their environment or their inner selves. Therefore, there is no resolution at the end of his plays. The drama critics, by and large, have failed to realize this.

## CHAPTER II

## BRIDIE'S CHOICE OF SUBJECTS

James Bridie, as we have seen, gives a vivid picture of the damaging effects of modern society on the human individual. In his dramas about non-conformists, he portrays the protagonists as men who are able to adjust to their environment and yet retain their peace of mind. In the plays concerning mental disease, however, the playwright delineates the corroding influence of non-conformity on mentally ill people.

The philosophy of being true to self is difficult to follow today because of the complete lack of objective values. The mentally ill tend to cut themselves off from society. As a result, their lives are not fruitful. As the patterns and techniques of social life alter, moral problems change their form so that the conventional answers to conventional questions no longer fit reality.

The modern world is full of contradictions. To what can a man be true?

The struggle in Bridie's plays highlights the dilemma facing contemporary man. His characters seem to indicate by their actions that integrity rooted in a sound estimate of human value is admirable but that an absence of values or distorted values will have fatal results for the individual struggling to retain a sense of identity.

Bridie's personal experience lies behind the dramatic world of his plays. The struggles of his life are reflected in them. A fuller knowledge of Bridie, the man, the doctor and the thinker, will clarify the kind of world that Bridie, the dramatist, creates in his drama. To his puritan upbringing he reacts with agnosticism, to his middle class environment he replied with social criticism. Many of the problems of adjustment that this author faced as a young man are absorbed into his experience and colour his thinking as a playwright in middle life.

First, we will examine the world into which Bridie was born. He was the eldest son of a successful Glasgow Marine engineer who had wanted to become a doctor. Lack of funds made this impossible and as a result he decided that his son would, whether he wished it or not, become a physician. Bridie's father was a strong willed non-practicing Presbyterian. This determination of his father was the first important event in Bridie's life. The strife between generations is discussed at length in "The Last Trump" and "Mr. Gillie".

Bridie (Osborne Henry Mavor) was born in 1888 while Queen Victoria was still on the throne and Britain was still expanding her overseas possessions. Like his father, he believed in progress, and in a set of standard beliefs which included the unquestioning obedience of children to their parents. Bridie was predestined for a medical career, and it mattered not if he were unsuited for this calling. The hopes and aspirations of Henry Mavor were to be fulfilled in his son. Bridie remained always a dutiful son. Yet his internal struggles and mental anguish may have resulted in his interest in various aspects of authority when he turned to writing his plays.

Bridie, like his protagonists, was a strong individualist. This, in part, may have been due to illness which during his formative years, excluded him from contact with his peers. He was never a robust child. He developed into a weak, small boy, stooping, spectacled, moody, and introverted, who spent much of his time reading in bed. His favourite books included the Bible, Shakespeare, "Pilgrim's Progress" and "The Cloister and the Hearth". Bridie informs us that as soon as his father noticed the first signs of intellectual stirring, he commenced reading aloud. Mavor senior read to his son Carlyle, Emerson, Robert Louis Stevenson, Tennyson, Browning, Coleridge, John Ruskin, Charles Darwin and "The Arabian Nights".

Another thing that made Bridie different from other boys of his middle class background was the increasing wealth of his parents. As the family moved into better and better residential districts of Glasgow, Bridie became more of a social outcast. When it came time to send him to school, he was first sent to the High School, but a year later he transferred to Glasgow Academy, a school for the sons of gentlemen of the upper classes. Bridie ruefully remarked:

> There was one enormous advantage in going to the Glasgow Academy of his day. One could confidently look to a respectable social position in the city. The principle common feature of its old boys seems to be that their souls remained unspotted by ten years of secondary education.[1]

This private school sent forth its students

to become Professors and Judges and Generals including several Field Marshals and even Proconsuls.

J.M. Barrie, the dramatist, had attended this school. In the social milieu in which the Mavor family now moved, the school tie with all its connotations had become of major importance in establishing a boy's position when the time came for him to face the world. As we shall see, Bridie in his work emphasizes a man's real worth, which is not solely based on his bank account or the reputation of the school which happened to have been chosen for him.

It was at Glasgow Academy that Bridie first showed his literary abilities as editor of the school magazine, "The Kernal". He illustrated his articles with delicate drawings and brilliant caricatures that revealed artistic promise. In later life, when he felt a play was not coming along as it should, he would throw it aside and start to paint or draw the difficult scene. But he chiefly enjoyed the writing and continued his literary pursuits during his years at Glasgow University.

Bridie was always sympathetic to the ordinary man, one of whom he considered himself. He did not have a distinguished academic career at University. He

followed his father's wishes and studied
medicine even though his heart was not
in it. He was fortunate, however, that
Scottish universities demanded all
science students to follow a strong Liberal Arts programme. Thus, Bridie
received a good broad education, reading
widely in the Classics and in English
Literature, besides being a regular con-
tributor to various literary journals. He
does not appear to have been upset at
failing his examinations. His father was
more concerned than Bridie that it took
him nine years to complete the medical
studies that would take only five for an
average student. His lack of academic
success in the field that had been selected
for him would indicate that he was in the
wrong profession. Yet, with persever-
ance, Bridie became a doctor at the age
of twenty-five.

During his father's life, Bridie never
openly opposed his wishes. He followed
the traditional ways of obedience. However, it is worth noting that the heroes
that he chose to portray in his plays are
non-conformists and rebels. They
attempt to do what Bridie himself never
did. They revolt against society, but the
result is disastrous for the individuals
concerned in most cases.

The influence of Henry Mavor over

his son lasted until his death, of pernicious anaemia, in 1915, at the early age of fifty-six. By then Bridie was in the mud of the trenches on the Western Front. The greatest single event of the dramatist's life was the Great War, 1914-1918. This was the holocaust, the hell that he had to go through and that utterly changed the world he had known as a young medical student.

The landscape in the background of all his plays is darkened by the remembrance of this four-year long blood-bath. August, 1914, saw Bridie in the uniform of the Royal Army Medical Corps. About a month later, Captain O.H. Mavor was in charge of an advance dressing station in Northern France, where he spent the next two years. In later years, he seldom mentioned this period of his life, dismissing it in his autobiography by saying: "We drifted from Ypres to Arras, to the Somme and back to Arras again."[2]

Eventually, his existence in the grim horror of the front line ended abruptly before the second battle of Arras, when he turned a bright orange and was sent home with a serious case of trench fever. While in France, Bridie acquired firsthand knowledge of the crippling mental effects of modern war on the minds of sensitive individuals. In France, too,

the young doctor handled more cases,
and of a wider variety, than many physicians deal with in their whole medical
career in peace time. [3]

The impressionable young doctor
could not but be affected by the suffering
and pain that surrounded him for two
years while serving on the Western Front.
Meanwhile, he was also conscious of the
corroding effect of the war on the
home front. The social structure of
British society, which is examined in his
plays, was undermined by the war. The
moral decay, depicted in T. S. Eliot's
"The Waste Land", forms the background
to Bridie's dramatic world. This background becomes even darker in hue as
the dramatist lives through and writes
about the blighting effects of the second
world-wide conflict of this century.

After spending several months in the
United Kingdom recovering from the
mental and physical strain of two years
under constant fire, Bridie was sent as
a replacement to the Middle East. This
assignment had a definite therapeutic
value for the war-weary doctor. He
travelled widely across the 'Fertile
Crescent', being stationed at different
times in Egypt, Persia, India and South-
ern Russia. He wrote a book about his
experiences in Persia, entitled "Some

Talk of Alexander" (1926) which was his
first literary endeavour and was a complete financial failure.

Travel always held a great fascination
for Bridie. In the world of his plays, his
heroes try to escape from their environment either by reading, as Mr. Gillie
does, or by travelling as Dr. Angelus
hoped to, and Dr. Mallaby in "The
Switchback" does. Persia is the earthly
paradise that the latter character is
seeking to escape to. Having been raised
as a Bible-reading Presbyterian, Bridie
examined the ruins of the ancient Middle
East with the earnestness of a trained
archaeologist.

Meanwhile, he continued to be an
observer of men, and of the effects of
their environment on them. Indeed, the
Biblical plays that he wrote later owe
part of their success to the faithfulness
of his detailed description of the setting,
obtained at first hand, and in keeping
with the scriptural accounts. It was while
Bridie was in the army that he gradually
acquired more outward going character-
istics, even though he was regarded as
a dour man by those who knew him well.

While overseas, he first became in-
tensely interested in people; previously
most of his knowledge of them had come
from books. His work as a medical

officer made him a keen observer of people as individuals, while his medical training inclined him to look at his patients as if they were guinea-pigs in a cage under permanent observation.

In later life when he became a playwright, Bridie continued to use clinical methods to describe his characters. We see his major protagonists as if they were patients with the doctor beside us, assisting us in diagnosing their particular mental ailments and the possible original causes.

At the end of the war, the well-travelled doctor, who had aspirations of a literary nature, bought a small Glasgow practice and joined the staff of the Victoria Infirmary as an assistant physician. Bridie soon discovered that he was not cut out temperamentally to be a general practitioner. As soon as it was financially possible, he gave up his private practice, spending all his energies at the large hospital. He was a gentle and sympathetic physician, respected and liked both by his colleagues and patients.

At this time, he commenced giving medical lectures, and worked arduously in a clinic for shell-shocked war veterans. He called on his personal experiences as a General Practitioner when he came to write about struggling young doctors in "The Switchback" and "Dr. Angelus".

It was almost by accident that Bridie
found his true vocation as a dramatist.
In the 1920's, even though he was living
a full and active life, something seems
to have been lacking. He felt that he was
drifting. He tells us what his feelings
were:

> Though my body and mind were fully
> occupied, my soul was a loose sheet
> flapping in the wind. Up to this point
> I had an uneasy suspicion that life
> was meaningless.[4]

He made a false start when drama-critic
Aflred Wareing rejected "The Switchback", saying it was clever, but that no
theatre manager would risk 'a brace of
buttons on it'. Bridie accepted this lone
verdict, put the manuscript aside, and
forgot all about his dreams of becoming
a playwright.

However, as his interest in the
theatre increased, his friend John Bradane[5] persuaded him to take an active
part in promoting a repertory company
known as the Scottish National Players.
In addition, Bradane introduced Bridie
to a literary group of Glasgow professional men who were attempting to discover new playwrights whose dramas
were on Scottish themes. He joined
Bradane as one of the directors of the

Scottish National Players, which had Tyrone Guthrie as its able young producer. With the encouragement of Bradane, Bridie wrote a farce-morality, "The Sunlight Sonata", which was produced in 1920.

This was the first of a remarkable series of plays that flowed from Bridie's pen. Now he commenced living a double life: Dr. O. H. Mavor continued his duties as a medical consultant during the day, and in the evening the dramatist took over, working into the small hours of the morning, writing and re-writing his dramas. Bridie was a very rapid worker, writing a total of forty plays besides attending to his other duties. His profession, not surprisingly, influenced his work as a dramatist. Indeed, many of his best drawn characters are doctors, and the problems that he deals with usually have medical overtones.

The real identity of Bridie, the dramatist, did not remain a secret for long. In 1930, he had a double triumph with the first production of "The Anatomist" in Edinburgh, and "Tobias and the Angel" at the Cambridge Drama Festival. It was common knowledge that their author was the well-known Glasgow physician.

"A Sleeping Clergyman", considered
by some his greatest play, had its premiere three years later at the Malvern
Festival. Bridie himself believed that
this curious play was the nearest thing
to a masterpiece that he wrote. It deals
with the ethics of the medical profession.
Bridie explains the play thus:

> In "A Sleeping Clergyman", I showed
> a wild horse after three generations
> or incarnations finally harnessing
> itself to the world for the world's
> good. God, who had set it all going,
> took his ease in an armchair through-
> out the play. The odd quality of the
> play made itself evident in rehearsal,
> the electricians, the stagehands, the
> wardrobe ladies, the charwomen in
> the theatre showed an interest in it
> from the start. [6]

In this unusual drama, the protagonist is
the creative urge itself. It flows through
the first to the third generations, sur-
viving the blighting influence of disease,
crime and debauchery of the second generation. The fulfilment of the rich promise of genius in Charles Cameron who
died young, is actualized in the life, dedicated to the service of mankind, of his
grandson and granddaughter when the
former produces a wonder drug and the

43

latter becomes the secretary-general of a world organization. This play points up one of Bridie's real fortes: that of creating realistic characters lsuch as Dr. Marshall, who come alive on the stage.

However, several of his plays, especially his light Scottish comedies, show lack of revision and technical flaws which are not surprising when we realize the speed at which they were produced by a man who was as busy as Bridie.

Finally, in 1938, he retired as a physician, and celebrated the event by having three new plays running in London at the same time. "The King of Nowhere" had its premiers at the Old Vic, with Laurence Olivier playing the part of Vivaldi, an aging actor of unbalanced mind; "Babes in the Wood" was produced at the Embassy, while "The Last Trump" was Bridie's offering at the Malvern Festival. This last play is a theraputical fantasia, concerning a hard-headed, and hard-hearted, Scottish financier who becomes a terrified hypochondriac until he believes the world is coming to an end. Bridie could not have written such a successful drama on this theme without calling upon his medical experience.

The retirement of Bridie from medicine was short. He was back in uniform as a doctor a couple of weeks after the outbreak of the Second World War in September, 1939. This time he did not serve overseas, but was working in London during the Blitz. Many theatres across the country closed down for the duration, but Bridie continued to write for those that remained open. Bridie went through a period of deep depression after the death of his fighter pilot son in action over Britain. However, he overcame his despondency and wrote "Mr. Bolfry", his best occult drama, which had its premiere in 1943.

After the war ended, Bridie retired for the second time from the practice of medicine. Thus once more, he could devote all his time and energy to playwriting, and to the development of 'live theatre' in Scotland. In the following year, the British government recognised his services in both the medical and literary fields by making him a Commander of the Order of the British Empire. Glasgow University, his 'Alma Mater', had previously given him an honorary Doctor of Laws degree.

In the years following the Second Worls War, Bridie wrote several of his most mature plays on the struggle between the individual and the conforming influences in society. He also played a vital role in the formation of the Glasgow

Citizens' Theatre.

In addition, he became one of the original promoters of the now famous Edinburgh International Festival for which he wrote "John Knox" (1947), a historical play about the reformation in Scotland. This is Bridie's historical lesson in over-dedication; in it Knox, who was in violent conflict with the society he found in Scotland on his return from the Continent, clearly summarized his own defect:

> I thought there was a man sent from Heaven whose name was John, but I took the ordinary road for getting here. It was ill luck that I got a voice that could talk kings off their thrones and I thought too much of it. [8]

The theme of the misdirected prophet was also central in Bridie's three versions of the biblical story of "Jonah and the Whale".

In the same year appeared "Dr. Angelus", which he based on a historical incident involving a Dr. Pritchard of Edinburgh in 1830, using documentary material to create a clinical investigation of an insane physician. "Daphne Laureola" (1949) and "Mr. Gillie" (1950) were the last two plays that Bridie wrote, in which he used his medical experiences to delineate the major characters. Both plays had long, successful London runs.

Although chiefly a study in contemporary disillusionment, "Daphne Laureola" also gives Bridie's best full-length portrait of a woman, Lady Katherine Pitts. Turning to "Mr. Gillie", we find possibly the simplest of all Bridie's plays. It is placed in a supernatural framework of the judgement after death of an unsuccessful Scottish village schoolmaster. Gillie is one of the great eccentrics that we find in Bridie's plays.

In the plays themselves, we note that there is no progression from a study of non-conformism to insanity. However, in his pre-World War II dramas, much more hope is expressed in man's future. The plays that he wrote in the post-war period, especially "Mr. Gillie", "Daphne Laureola" and "Dr. Angelus", are much more gloomy. The world that Bridie shows us in these plays is full of despair. His major characters cannot adjust to society.

It will become more evident as we proceed that the personal world of Bridie lies behind and clarifies the dramatic world, as we see it, in his plays. There is a definite unity in the dramatic works which deal with the same problems facing modern man. He focuses his attention on the condition of the social misfit, but offers no ready solution for obtaining adjustment. This will become apparent from a closer examination of the plays.

The argument of "The Switchback", his first full-length play, revolves around the discovery of a humble but brilliant country doctor who is thwarted by higher professionalism. When the Medical Council changes its attitude, he refuses their offer in Timon-like scorn, rejects civilisation, and leaves for the Asian desert to find communion with the dead past and "the infinites of space".

This play exemplified one of Bridie's most detached efforts. At no time does he sacrifice in it the serious idea of his theme to exhibit his wit and humour. As we shall see in the next chapter, the situation arises out of character conflict. His protagonist is caught up in his environment. Bridie knew from personal experience, while practicing medicine in Glasgow, the power of institutions in hamstringing the creative urge of the individual

The power of finance is represented in the play by an unscrupulous Jewish businessman while that of the mass media by an equally unprincipled newspaper proprietor. Bridie said the play was intended to demonstrate the Vanity of

Human Wishes, the Importance of Being Earnest, the Inevitability of Fate, the Economic Law, the Immortality of the Soul, and the Pleasure of Hope.[9]

The play does point to t h e problems facing modern man, a physician in this case, who tries to remain true to his principles while the forces around him attempt to corrupt him. There is no sign of the apprentice playwright in this play. Bridie, possibly because he became a dramatist late in life, matured as a playwright almost overnight.

The strife theme was still engrossing Bridie twentyfive years l a t e r w h e n he wrote "Mr. Gillie". This study of a village schoolmaster's remote and unsung career is probably Bridie's best integrated play, for here his characteristic b r i l l i a n c e is perfectly matched with humanity. Here, the author condemns the opportunistic profiteering in post-war Britain.

Although o n e is a schoolmaster and the other a doctor, the character of Gillie is like that of the protagonist in "The Switchback". This suggests that Bridie, in one sense, spent his whole writing career examining one man and his possible way of life. The same protagonist appears again a n d again in his work but in each play the spotlight catches and reveals him in the s a m e struggle but in a different setting.

Here the struggle centres about an unselfish man, who is in the world, but will not compromise his principles in order to be accepted by it. A comparison of these two plays shows that his methods did not change radically, In each of them, dramatic unity has been achieved by focusing on the problems facing one character.

Bridie's first almost clinical examination of mental disease was in "The Last Trump" (1938) The protagonist can no longer function effectively in his society because of his lust for power and fear of death. The conflict theme dominates the drama which discusses the moral problems facing the modern captains of industry. The protagonist is only saved from the blighting effects of his lust by a traumatic experience.

A much less optimistic view of life is depicted in "Daphne Laureola" (1949). This play is completely nihilistic. The individual fails in his struggle with a grim materialistic society. In this play the characters seem to have a hollow centre because they have abandoned all traditional values and replaced them with nothing they can believe in. Here, we get a glimpse of Bridie's meaningless Hell. There is a definite traceable downward progression in the plays which concern man's future. In this, his work mirrors the age he was living in. Again the theme of conflict between the individual and society gives a focus to the drama. The play is one of human loneliness, despondency and gloom.

Critics have attacked "Daphne Laureola" for apparent lack of structure, saying that it consists of three brilliant first acts. They have failed to realize that the dramatist constructed the play so in order to develop the basic conflict. This play aptly catches the spirit of defeatism and hopelessness that was prevalent in Britain during the later 1940's.

As has been previously observed, Bridie was intrigued by the amoral attitudes of the criminal, especially medical physicians who become involved with murder. To Bridie, it would appear from a close study of his plays, murderers were persons whose actions, due to some form of mental disorder, harm not only themselves but the society which produced them. The theme of conflict between the doctor and society dominates Bridie's two dramas dealing with murder. Although "The Anatomist" (1930) is set in nineteenth century Edinburgh, the problems discussed are those of our modern urban society. The plays examine the ethics of the medical profession.

The protagonist in "The Anatomist" is based on a historical figure, Dr. Robert Knox, who was involved with a gang of grave-robbers and murderers. The play does not deal with the more sensational aspects of the source material, but concentrates on the dilemma the physician faces himself. He must have bodies for his students to work on, and does not concern himself with how they are obtained. The protagonist claims he is a searcher after truth, and that truth can be found in the accumulation of facts. [10] Here, we are faced with the old problem of does the end, in this case pushing back the frontiers of scientific knowledge, justify the means, which is murder.

The final play to be examined, "Dr. Angelus" (1947), is based on the Glasgow case of the notorious Dr. Pritchard, who was executed for the murder of his mother-in-law and wife in the eighteen-thirties. The dramatist in updating the play by one hundred years has cunningly fused the two periods so that the lingering remnants of Victorianism, as expressed in the setting itself and in the characters of the victims, produce an atmosphere in which a megalomaniac of the nineteen-twenties can operate with effective theatre.

In order to emphasize the strife that Bridie saw in contemporary society, he selected certain types of characters to examine in his plays. These characters illustrate the dramatist's preoccupation with the non-conformist. In the following chapters, we will study the major plays of James Bridie to see how his protagonists adjust or fail to adjust to twentieth century society.

The merely non-conformist heroes are seen in "The Switchback" and "Dr. Gillie". Both are professional men — Dr. Mallaby, a country doctor, and Gillie, a rural school teacher. They strive against the corroding influences of society. They may be failures in the eyes of the world, but to themselves they are free and unconquered.

On the other hand, the mentally-ill protagonists that dominate "The Last Trump" and "Daphne Laureola" cut themselves off from society, and cannot live fruitful and satisfying existences. The hero of the former play is cured by living through a traumatic experience. In the latter play, Lady Pitts is drifting to easeful death. She has given up the fight.

The final group of plays, "The Anatomist" and "Dr. Angelus", deals with murderers who are not only cut off from society, but turn and attack the social structure itself. Bridie's choice of characters and the way in which he develops them strengthens his major thesis in his work. The short-comings of contemporary British society are shown by their effect on a few individuals. Bridie focuses his attention on the maladjusted person. His scope is narrow, yet he takes his audience step by step along the path chosen by his heroes. His characters develop from the fight between the individuals and the encroachments of society on individual freedom of action.

# CHAPTER III

## THE NON-CONFORMIST HEROES

One cannot but feel that what the everyday world often considers as a non-conformist is to James Bridie the 'real man'. He portrayed Dr. Mallaby in "The Switchback" as a person who follows the dictates of his own conscience. He appears to sympathize with the country doctor's rebellious actions because he realized that many of the accepted conventions and norms of modern society are false. Bridie had no use for the grey conformist who often must become a hypocrite and compromise himself in order to get ahead in a worldly way. He seems to be trying to show us that a strong individualist, like Dr. Mallaby, can survive if he remains true to self.

The argument of "The Switchback" revolves around the new discovery of a humble but brilliant doctor who is thwarted by the higher professionalism of the Medical Council. When its attitude changes, he refuses its offer of an expensive laboratory to carry out his ex-

periments. He rejects what civilization
has to offer and leaves "for the Asian
vastness to find communion with the dead
past and the infinite of space".[1]

The play opens in Dr. Mallaby's
library and general workroom in his
isolated home on a Scottish Moor. The
young doctor, like Bridie, has gone
through the crucible of the Great War in
the trenches of Northern France, and is
now on the point of perfecting a cure for
tuberculosis. He has already cured one
patient but his experiments and researches are necessarily slowed up by
the demands of his practice. Three
strangers whose car has broken down
are welcomed by the doctor's pretty wife
in the middle of the night. They identify
themselves as Sir Anthony Craye, the
president of the Royal Academy of Medicine and Surgery; Lord Pascal, the
Publisher of a chain of daily newspapers;
and Mr. Abraham Burmeister, a Jewish
gentleman interested in finance. They
represent the outside world of power to
the struggling doctor.

However, Aunt Dinah, a mildly demented canny Scottish woman, immediately recognizes their selfish shallow-
ness. She interprets Pascal as "a rascal",
the Jewish businessman as "bucket-shop",
and the great abdominal surgeon as "Cray

fish". All three modern exploiters of the masses are susceptible to the charms of Mrs. Mallaby. They also discover that the country doctor is an unusual fellow by the books, ranging from Charles Doughty's "Arabia Deserta" to the latest works on various fields of medicine, they find in the room. Their lack of principles is seen in their going through the absent physician's private papers. They find out that Dr. Mallaby is working on a new cure for tuberculosis. Sir Anthony is impressed in spite of his patronizing attitude to "only another cure". Nevertheless, he dismisses the researches as being worthless because Mallaby is personally unknown to him, and because he is not using the latest expensive equipment. Sir Anthony's narrow-minded views, and unwillingness to accept new ideas is all too common in the modern professional organisations which Bridie is attacking.

The surgeon's two companions immediately see the work of the young doctor in its potentiality for increasing their own large fortunes — Lord Pascal is interested in it as a sensational news story that may boost the circulations of his newspapers, while Mr. Burmeister sees the cure as a potential source of wealth through promotion.

By the time Dr. Mallaby appears on the stage, the two businessmen are ready to offer him a splendid, new, fully equipped research clinic and ample funds for him to continue his work in London. Mallaby, who is described as a mild little man in a bowler hat, a threadbare coat, carrying a battered black bag, is not impressed by his visitors, or by their offers of friendship and assistance. The beautiful yet shallow Mrs. Mallaby begs and bullies her husband to accept what she sees as a golden opportunity to escape from the lonely moors of Scotland. At the same time, Aunt Dinah prophesies that the project is doomed to failure, and predicts that her neice will run off with one of the crooked businessmen.

Thus, Dr. Mallaby, an innocent, selfless student in the cause of humanity, is surrounded by individuals who represent the expediency characterizing our civilization. He is not wise in the ways of the world. Bridie portrays Mallaby as a dedicated hard-working General Practitioner who reads "Paradise Lost" in his few spare moments. He is not interested in finding a cure to relieve human suffering and pain. He recognises Sir Anthony for what he really is — "a pompous ass". Mallaby is an earnest Presbyterian who never laughs at anyone — but himself: "Life's too serious".

However, he is no match for the machinations of Lord Pascal and Mr. Burmeister. He ignores prophetic warnings of Aunt Dinah who is his only true friend. Bridie uses the mildly demented aunt to foreshadow the later events in the play. Aunt Dinah, a Casandra-like figure, is fated not to be taken seriously by the other people in the drama. As we shall see, this is also the fate of Mr. Gillie in the play of that name.

Mallaby is contrasted with his three visitors, Sir Anthony has been tainted with a thirst for power. Mr. Burmeister is a slave to money, while the recently created peer from Fleet Street wants to cash in on the journalistic aspects of Mallaby's discovery. The doctor realizes that it is much too soon to make any announcements regarding his tuberculosis researches. He tells his wife that he wants his work to stand by itself "without assistance from distinguished and benevolent boobs".

His researches are still in the preliminary stages and he only hopes to complete his work in his lifetime. He knows that there are years of controlled experiments and verifications still to do on his tuberculosis cure. However, he is not dismayed at this prospect. He is content to continue his researches in his spare time from his other medical duties.

But Dolly Mallaby is not! It is she who tempts Mallaby. The two business-men back her up while Sir Anthony auto-cratically vetoes the whole scheme. Mallaby is infuriated by Sir Anthony's attitude, and goaded beyond endurance by his ambitious young wife. The opport-unities for a speed-up of his researches are too much. Dr. Mallaby finally accepts the business proposition, certain that the magnitude of his discovery will give him the power to keep his integrity, and keep the press accounts clean of any cheapening sensationalism.

Here we see a Bridian hero, a non-conformist by nature, being seduced by society. By accpeting the assistance of Pascal and Burmeister, he, in fact, be-comes their prisoner. He is no longer a free agent. "The Switchback" is one of Bridie's most detached efforts, and at no time does he sacrifice the serious idea of his theme to a mere exhibition of wit and humour. The dramatist focuses his attention on Dr. Mallaby who makes a grave mistake by becoming mixed up with his London visitors.

The second act opens in a London hotel where the little doctor is completely out of his element. He has failed to con-trol the newspaper proprietor and the financier who have exploited him for their own selfish ends. Lord Pascal's papers have distorted all his statements to make them as sensational as possible. Mallaby realizes that he has been duped, and made to look like a cheap publicity-hungry quack. But it is already too late.

The all-powerful Medical Council is moving against Dr. Mallaby for what it terms unethical conduct in giving his research findings to the press. The young doctor reaffirms to his backers that his tuberculosis cure is still only in the experimental stages. He attempts to remain honest. However, Lord Pascal ignores Mallaby's personal views, and goes on to use him as a political football in his quest for power.

The strain becomes almost too much for Mallaby. His mind is in a whirl. He complains to his wife that the atmosphere of London, and the shady dealings of Messrs. Pascal and Burmeister, remind him of the horrors of the late war: "You can't describe it, but it's a sort of hot sickness. Disgusting! And you wish you'd never come. I wish I had never come." His wife, who has been blinded by greed and the flattery of rich gifts from Burmeister, is no help to Mallaby. All she does is accuse him of not having a thick enough skin. She believes that he is bound to win, remarking:

> You would have liked to fight the
> Germans in full armour with an Um-
> pire to see that both sides kept the
> rules of chivalry, but you just had to
> do what a coarse-grained General
> told you, because he knew how to
> fight Germans and you don't.

Mallaby, like so many who survived
physically the horrors of the 1914-1918
war, murmurs in reply that he wonders
if the Generals really did know how to
fight the Germans.

But Mallaby, the individualist, is
fighting a losing battle against the immoral men who surround him. He discovers too late that Burmeister has stolen
his brainless wife, that he has lost his
good name as a doctor due to Pascal's
machinations, and that Sir Anthony has
had his name struck off the medical
Register when it appears there is a flaw
in his cure. Mallaby is a ruined man.
The little Scottish doctor is the scape-
goat and society makes him an outcast.

In the third act we find Mallaby
drinking hard and completely disillusioned about modern society. Dishonoured,
he has gone back to Aunt Dinah who stands
by him. He is the victim of Lord Pascal's
newspaper stunt. What opulent inter-

ference and undue haste had made manifest in a streamlined clinic on which the impudent search-light of gaudy publicity has been turned, the patient struggling, back-room efforts of the country doctor, left to himself, might have made eradicable in God's time. Altruism has been seduced by the shoddy artifices of civilization. That is Bridie's theme in this powerful drama.

Sir Anthony shows up with penitent Dolly Mallaby who got as far as Nuremburg before getting fed-up with Burmeister. The proud Sir Anthony offers Mallaby his friendship. The surgeon wants Mallaby to come and work for him because he now realizes the real worth of the brilliant young doctor and wants to be associated with any future discoveries Mallaby might make. But the ex-doctor, aided by Aunt Dinah, scornfully rejects the surgeon's offer. Instead, Mallaby and Aunt Dinah join forces and decide to go to Palmyra to dig up relics of past civilizations. He declares:

> The only practical things are life and eternity. I'll go where they've written their message on the grey face of the world. I'm free, I tell you. Free. The bonds of my captivity are broken. I'll go now. As far as I can. Nothing a man does with his whole soul is ever lost.

Thus, does Mallaby turn on Sir Anthony as a freed convict might turn on the man whose circumstantial evidence has put him behind bars when that same witness' revelation of the deeper truth might have saved "the prisoner" and his work.

It is the logical ending, eccentric though it seems at face value. By making Mallaby drunk in the third act, Bridie lost sympathy for his central character, according to drama critics. The deposed doctor makes a passionate indictment of a society led by materialistic newspaper magnates. But Mallaby, after all, has a sorrow sizeable enough to justify his taking to the bottle and Bridie does make Mallaby talk himself out of the alcoholic bluster into a raving sobriety. All this third act needed was an astringent. Mallaby talks dynamically but he talks too much.

The main dissatisfaction of the critics with this last act was that it s e e m e d to be alien to the character of the first two acts. In Act III, Bridie abandons naturalism, changing into a crazy rhythm to harmonize with Aunt Dinah; making her mistress of ceremonies. But Aunt Dinah's form of madness is simply that of speaking the truth, of disclaiming the magnates' bribes, of seeing through them, and of seeing through the s e l f i s h n e s s of Sir

Anthony. She has every right to inspire
Mallaby with the madness of truth in the
last act. The naked truth so rarely sur-
faces in civilized society that it has the
effect of freakishness when it does so.
The naturalistic alternative in tune with
ACTS I and II would probably have projectec
a distraught Mallaby having a final outburst
against the calumnies of fate, and then a
sobered Mallaby turning over a new page
of research and quietly beginning
again with still greater odds against him.
This would be a pathetic finale, alien in
feeling to the first two acts, with Aunt
Dinah's gay and ingenious outbursts as the
ravings of a lunatic instead of the rich and
strange channels of truth.

Aunt Dinah, who is embarrassingly
frank in speech, is the dominant character in the final scenes of the drama.
She, in her non-conformity, has a lot in
common with Dr. Mallaby. It is she more
than alcohol that brings out the poetic
side of the down-trodden physician. And
Mallaby gives a powerful description of
the world that he has decided to quit:

..... Craye, you've cast me out of
     your civilization and found a niche
     for me again in it. I can see your
     civilization piled terrace on terrace,
gallery on gallery, with the dumb,

carved figures of the damned writhing
around its pedestal. Up and up and
up it goes to the clouds, where you
and Pascal and Burmeister walk in
state with other priests and pedants
and princes and judges and money-
lenders and magicians. You walk very
proudly in the scarlet gowns the universities gave you for your importance
and magnificence and your usefulness.
You made this monument, you made
this memorial, pulling out here and
pushing in there, this man's life work
and that woman's pain. You laid the
lash on the backs of the slaves till it
grew and grew. Beautiful. Immense.
Almost perfect. A little more, a
little arranging, a few more tired
men's lives worked into the arabesque
and the thing will be complete. Oh,
a tower, a palace, a world fit for
surgeons and financiers and newspaper proprietors to live in!

We can see that Mallaby has matured
during the play. He has passed through
the inferno and is now on the calm of
Mount Purgatorio. He has broken the
chains that held him to a society with
which he had so little in common. He
has refused to become a slave in Cray's
treadmill, grinding out a few false proofs

to bolster up the ephemeral superstitions
of pundits. He turns his back on Britain,
and goes into the east where
    there'll be generation after generation
    to talk to. Dead men tell no tales?
What rot! Dead men do nothing else
but tell tales all day long and all night
long. Ironic tales.

Mallaby's line, "Nothing a man does with
his whole soul is ever lost", is a recurring
Bridie theme and a good note on which to
end the play.
    It is worth noting that James Bridie
had spent two years (1917-1919) among
the ruins of the lost civilizations of the
Middle East. It was while he was here,
that he recovered his own peace of mind
after the harrowing years as an army
doctor in France. There is a sincerity
about this play's end which gives it an
added dimension.
    The sole character in "The Switch-
back" that is not convincingly drawn by
Bridie is Mrs. Mallaby. She has not
enough personality to make four men out
of four men fall in love with her. Bridie's
own description of this character in a
letter to Edward MacRoberts is worth
quoting:

. . . . . . . Mrs. Mallaby is a very tall,

pretty, scatter-brained person who has not even begun to adapt herself to real life. She has drifted into the Mallaby menage from exactly the same motives, or lack of them, as she drifts out of it. [2]

That kind of woman serves Bridie's purpose as a contrast to the intense, purposeful Mallaby, but it is a make-up lacking feminine magnetism and vitality and would simply bore those men of wealth, power and influence who knock on her door in the middle of the night.

The first two acts of this thought-provoking play state a problem belonging to modern civilization. However, we know enough about Bridie's method and approach not to expect any resolution of the problem in the final act. Naturally, an audience which wants a problem solved is disappointed in "The Switchback". The dramatist has presented to us some rather uncomfortable truths about contemporary society and how a man who refuses to conform is crushed. However, Mallaby is not destroyed. He escapes by travelling away to Palmyra, accompanied by his wife and Aunt Dinah.

Mr. Gillie, Bridie's other great non-conformist, cannot escape from civilization so easily. In many ways, the char.

acter of the Scottish schoolmaster is similar to that of Dr. Mallaby.

In "Mr. Gillie", Bridie probes the career of a village schoolmaster. This is possibly Bridie's best play, for here his character brilliance is perfectly matched with humanity. For once he has gone as deep with emotion as he ever went high with wit. The action mounts with a fine sense of form; character here is not to be so replete with cleverness that some sympathy must be sacrificed. "Mr. Gillie" succeeds abundantly as a parable and as an example of how the author could write a domestic drama. It is the only play of its kind in his entire collection; it is also the simplest of all his plays.

The hero of the title is a complete failure in the eyes of the world. Gillie, nevertheless, is not a failure to himself and Bridie shows us that the modern standards of success, which are sub-scribed to by the other characters, are false. This play is a type of tragi-comedy. The playwright has set the main action of the drama between a brief allegorical prologue and an epilogue in which a heavenly judge is trying Mr. William Wotherspoon Gillie as a possible cand-idate for immortality. Prior to this pro-logue, the country school teacher had been killed by a furniture van hired to remove all his possessions to the auction room, after he had been declared bankrupt.

The scene in Heaven fades and the story of Mr. Gillie unfolds, at the same time revealing one of the social tragedies of our time. Mr. Gillie is an obscure philosopher. He is a completely unselfish, dedicated, patient dominie who is as autocratic as Nature itself in commanding green shoots from the infinitesimal spaces between the stones sown by a barren, materialistic society. He is in the world, but will not be a part of it. He has spent his life as a teacher in an isolated mining community "Opening cages and letting prisoners fly free." 3 His sole aim is to develop the creative spark in his students. He preaches to them the poverty of riches and the wealth of the imagination.

The play proper begins Gillie's story, at a critical moment of his life when he learns from the Reverend Gibb, chairman of the education committee, that his school is to be closed and that he is to take a subordinate position in another school under a headmaster whom he dislikes. Gillie immediately resigns and begins to write a novel, his second in twenty years. Thus, we see his inde-

pendent spirit. He is not overly concerned
with security or even promotion within
the school system.  He would have been
a writer years before if he could, and
not a teacher of English. His philosophy
about writing explains his kindness; "if
I can't., I'll help others that can." His
first novel, which had been published by
an Edinburgh firm, sold only four hundred
and forty-six copies. It brought him in
seven pounds, five and eightpence half-
penny. Since then, he had given up
serious writing, but had made "nearly
forty pounds a year by writing science
notes for "The Boy's Companion". Mrs.
Gillie believed that her husband could
have been the headmaster of a big school
in Glasgow if he had only paid attention
to his "cards".

Instead, he carefully watched his
pupils, all the while waiting for a few
capable ones to become inspired.  These
students he filled with enthusiasm; these,
too, he unsettled by widerning their intellectual horizons. Gillie explains:
"Thank the Lord for that. If I've done
nothing else in my life, at least I've unsettled one or two people." To these few
able students he gave "the key to the
treasure houses and taught the mysteries."

On the day Gillie resigns from the
school board, he learns that his latest

protege, a miner's son, has decided to leave for London where he hopes to become a playwright. The youth, Tom Donnelly, is rather conceited, and one feels that he is not altogether worthy of the individual attention his teacher has bestowed on him. It is revealed that Tom has married the daughter of the local doctor, who is an alcoholic. Tom's young bride, Molly Watson, is another of Gillie's more promising students. The schoolmaster is accused by his wife, Dr. Watson and the local Presbyterian minister, of encouraging and promoting the marriage of the two young people. He is accused of betraying the trust the parents have placed in him.

Gillie is one of the three most prominent people in the village of Crult. However, he does not support the views of the minister and the doctor. They feel that he is a traitor to the establishment by inculcating new ideas into the heads of his students. Rev. Gibb, who is also the chairman of the schoolboard, and Dr. Watson represent the same forces in society that Dr. Craye, Lord Pascal and Mr. Burmeister did in "The Switchback". They want Gillie to compromise the principles to which he has held all his life. The schoolmaster shows inner fortitude by his support of the newly wedded couple, even though he scolds them for being too precipitate. He declares:

> We've just had an example of guts and determination; and that's one thing none of us here h a s shown for many a long day. You ought to be proud of your flock, Mr. Gibb. You ought to be proud too, Watson, if there's a spark of pride in y o u r sodden composition..... I feel enormously uplifted. I've just had a glimmer of an intimation that life's worth living. ... Did you ever know an artist who was any good who wasn't prepared to b u r n down his house and go out like a Man after his Grail?

Thus, Gillie feels that his twenty-five years have not been wasted teaching in this small backward community. Long ago he realized that he was no genius himself. However, he hopes to fulfil his o w n aspirations by helping others to utilize their God-given creative gifts. But his associates and neighbours in Crult do not understand him. To them, his attitude appears very strange, and quite eccentric. They look on him as a dangerous man w h o is a disturbing influence on the re mote mining community.

Every character in the play is well

drawn. Mr. Gillie himself, a rugged individualistic dominie of the old school, is Bridie's most lovable portrait, n o t excluding the biblical portraits in "Tobias and the Angel" and "Susannah and the Elders". He follows his own peculiar temperament or bent. H i s deviations from customary behaviour as represented by the selfishness of the minister and doctor are clearly s e e n and understood by the audience. He is normal, even though the community looks on him as an eccentric. His actions, like those of D r. M a l l a b y in "The Switchback", are not dominated by self-inter st.

He has devoted his life to bring forth the best in his pupils. He attempts to turn "geese into swans". But he admits that most of his former proteges, including Johnny Caw, Charlie Wishart and Willie MacIntyre, have failed him. However, Gillie is philosophical about his failures: "There's no way of telling a weak character till it's up against life." This is because the human soul is not like anything e l s e and anything we do about it is not like anything else. Gillie's insights into human nature are much greater than t h o s e of the clergyman or the physician, who time and again accuse him of escaping from his duties and responsibilities. He maintains that he has a higher responsibility than to his employers and the community. Gillie also observes that there is only one kind of man who is not ordered about from the cradle to the grave:

> .....and that's the artist. He is bullied like the rest; but he's under nobody's orders. He's responsible to God and perhaps to his neighbours. But not to what you call the community, I'd be an artist myself if I could. If I can't, I will help others to be that. And you and the rest of you can do what you like about it.

This is the brave declaration of independence of the middle-aged teacher. Mr. Gillie is the character that appears to really fascinate his creator in this play. Bridie draws him as a 'well-rounded' character with unfathomed depths.

Other characters that appear in the first act of "Mr. Gillie" are well drawn. Mrs. Gillie is a warm-hearted wife, commonsensical, but with enough of uncommon common sense to have sensibility. She is a worthy mate for the small Scottish schoolmaster. Dr. Watson, Nelly's alcoholic humbug of a parent, is a clever study of a selfish weak, possessive father. Bridie invested his portrait of the rural general practitioner with sentimentality. There is a mental poverty in the doctor's statements, and in his selfish whining for his daughter whom he treats merely as a household drudge. Mr. Gibb, the minister, whose duty it is to dismiss Gillie as an unsuitable experimental guide for the young, is sufficiently conventional and expedient to highlight the schoolmaster's greater claim to grace. And Tom and Nelly, the young people who owe their mentor so much, are tremendously alive; they both have a strain of violent egotism which Bridie handles well in the first act, and goes on to develop in the second.

For example, Tom's rather rude and indolent attitude towards Gillie in the opening scene of the play, prepares us for the second act which takes place six months later. Gillie's confidence has again been misplaced. This is clearly seen with the return of Tom, the would-be playwright, and his wife from London. They have both let him down. They fail from lack of moral stamina. Nelly has not touched her violin for months, and has become little more than a 'call-girl', while her husband has forgotten all his dreams and plans of becoming a Man of Letters. Tom has given up the ambitions that his master had conceived for him, and has become a 'spiv'. [4] He is an ex-

ecutive assistant to a Mr. Kelly, a shady
London businessman, who has "his hooks
on the dogs and slot machines and tele-
vision and real estate and roadhouses
and night clubs". Nelly is Kelly's part-
time mistress, a fact that does not offend
her husband who has amassed a fortune
of five thousand pounds in his half year
sojourn in London.

On his return, Tom commences to
give literary advice to Gillie. He is giving
Gillie advice on how to improve his writing style. Tom feels his master's re-
dundancy might be avoided if Gillie would
only bend to a course of pep-and-drive,
which should turn the dull, old-fashioned
novels he writes into selling propositions.
The argument here is brilliant satire,
Mr. Gillie's rapier to Tom's toy sword.

Tom also runs down the great men of
the past, including John Milton, Robert
Browning, John Ruskin, and Thomas
Carlyle, saying: "This English Literature stuff is all hooey". Thus we see
that Tom's character has not been strong
enough for him to keep hold of the principles and set of values taught him by
Gillie. He has taken the easy way out
and has accepted the world on its own
terms and thinks only of himself. Tom's
character is contrasted with that of his
mentor who gladly gives up all to remain

true to the dictates of his own soul.

However, Gillie does not join the Reverend Gibb in his protests against Tom's views of English Literature. The narrow-minded minister declares pompously that "we are greatly indebted to literature which contributes towards character building, and which guides us through the thickets of existence". Gillie maintains, on the other hand, that literature builds nothing: "We owe it nothing. It forms nothing. It holds out nothing. It's as likely as not to guide us into the ditch. Literature and Art are God Almighty thinking aloud".

Here Gillie expresses his individualistic liberal creed which sees some good in all things. The little schoolmaster has matured through hardship and loss, but has not become bitter. He merely pities his former protégé and forgives his disrespectful outbursts. He has been mastered by something beyond self, by a true appreciation and understanding of life, literature and art.

If Mr. Gillie has made the wrong decision at every turn, he is, nevertheless, fundamentally in the right. The Procurator in the epilogue sums up the case against his application for immortality; Gillie's life story is one of misdirected effort. The public prosecutor declares that a man's work must be judged by the results it produces, and that Gillie "has done nothing and whatever influence he has exercised has been dissipated into absurdity or worse". He feels the eccentric schoolmaster should be consigned to limbo. The celestial judge, however, disagrees. He says:

> I find that this man devoted his life to opening cages and letting prisoners fly free. It was not his fault if the cat got the prisoners in the end. .....I find that most good men are occupied in designing and strengthening cages. I do not like cages. I think that the few minutes between the door of the cage and the jaws of the cat make life worth living.

The judge goes on to explain that whether Gillie's endeavours were useful or not is a matter for whoever gave him his instructions. Victory or defeat have nothing to do with the case. Let us at least be gentlemen. Let us honour the forlorn hope. The judge assigns William Gillie, the faithful servant of intellectual idealism, to the vacant seat between Lincoln and John Wesley in heaven. It appears that Bridie is telling us not to pass final judgement on Gillie's actions. The Instruction-Giver in the final analysis must be the sole judge, because only He knows the purpose behind Gillie's life.

In choosing the way of forlorn hope rather than acceptance or compromise, the Scottish dominie has literally chosen to slay himself to be himself. Gillie's behaviour is inherently ambigious. He has chosen the way of dedication, responsibility and selflessness, yet he attacks servility and conventional conceptions of responsibility. At the same time he is charged by his associates with being irresponsible and selfish. He is committed to inspiring the human soul of his students, and would die rather than fail to perform his duty. He explains to his wife that "if I'd seen those qualities and done less than my damndest to give them a chance, it would have been better for me to put a millstone round my neck and jump into the loch". Despite 'failures' Gillie goes on trying. He dies trying. Striving is what counts, not specific achievements.

Gillie plays a game of chess with Tom in the first act and loses. This game requires "an infinite capacity for taking pains". The schoolmaster loses because his wife's conversation interferes with his powers of concentration. Act II begins with Gillie winning a game of cribbage, a game of chance. Gillie's life is based upon the theory of chance — the winning of games of chance depends upon possession by the gods.

Further, Gillie believes that character is tested by chance and there is no way of telling a weak character till it is up against life. He took a chance on Tom and made a mistake. His final reflection is: "I was only wrong. There's nothing final about making mistakes — if there's no real harm done". No real harm has been done. Tom is a failure, even though the village of Crult feels that he has made a successful career for himself in London. Dr. Watson and Reverend Gibb feel that Gillie is completely wrong in grieving that Tom has turned into a spiv and that Nelly has become a quite expensive tart. The doctor is impressed that his son-in-law and daughter can afford first-class sleepers, hire a Rolls-Royce, wear flashy clothes, and live in an expensive London apartment. On the other hand, the minister is won over as a vocal supporter of the young people, when he learns that Tom has a large bank account. He fails in his duty as a man of God in not censoring the loose living and lack of morals of the young couple. It is ironic that both the minister and doctor apologise to Gillie, saying that he was right all the time. But Gillie sees further than either of his materialistic associates and realizes that his proteges are living in a spiritual wasteland.

The play proper ends with Gillie's rejecting offers of assistance from Tom and Gibb: his mind is already occupied with another promising pupil. "All she needs is a bit of encouragement", Gillie says, "I'll raise the de'il in her tomorrow". Thus, he goes on seeking to open the doors of locked cages.

Bridie has a fine appreciation of human values in his drawing of the character of the protagonist. Though the world seems to conspire against G i l l i e and he loses first his school and then his house, and he is due to fall ignominiously under the van that is removing his furniture to the sale room, he is a happy man. Not an idiotically happy man who does not feel his blows, but one whose understanding of the geography of life is not affected by the removal of landmarks and temporary shifting of signposts. When the final curtain falls, we are immersed in that unwritten Act that every great play leaves in its wake - awakened consciousness.

As has been stated, Bridie was concerned with individuals, and was aware of the corrupting influences of materialism on modern man. In these two plays, he has shown that his sympathies are with men who are strong enough to stand up against the forces in society which are demanding that all conform. Both Dr. Mallaby and Mr. Gillie ignore the advice of their friends, and follow the dictates of their own consciences. They have both opposed the false norms of society, but still are sane, not having distorted reality. In the eyes of the world the deposed doctor and the jobless teacher may be failures. However, both of them have integrity and an unshaken faith in mankind.

In the final analysis, the protagonists in these two plays justify their earthly existence: they have a kind of individualism that is based on inner conviction and peace of mind. We shall now turn to characters who are struggling for self identity, but who have none of the inner convictions of Mallaby and Gillie. They suffer from mental disorders and cut themselves off from living full lives. They cannot find contentment by conforming to the superficial values of their contemporaries.

Unlike Dr. Mallaby and schoolmaster Gillie, they do not possess an inner harmony which would enable them to persist as integrated individuals. In these dramas, James Bridie, physician-turned- playwright, takes us, as it were, on a conducted tour of the phychological ward of a mental institution and in a clinical fashion draws our attention to social misfits who are unable to adjust to modern society.

# CHAPTER IV

## THE MENTALLY-ILL PROTAGONISTS

In his plays about non-conformists, Bridie, as we noted, is interested in describing and delineating the curbing effects of modern urban society on the human individual. Now in his plays concerning mental illness, he shows the damaging results of eccentricity carried beyond that of the individualism of Mallaby and Gillie. The philosophy of being faithful to one's principles is difficult today because of the complete lack of recognition of objective values: Modern Man is the measure of all things. The problem is in what can man put his trust. Bridie's plays appear to indicate that being true to self to the point of being merely a non-conformist is sometimes necessary. However, other kinds of individualism may produce serious mental and emotional harm.

What determines the line of demarcation between oddness and mental illness

is hard to discover. The hope that is
apparent in Bridie's earlier dramas
dwindles as he grew older and Europe
moved towards the Second World War.
However, Bridie remained interested in
psychological problems and the conflicting interests of the individual and society
in the modern world. "The Last Trump"
(1938) is Bridie's first careful examination of paranoia. The symptoms of the
mental disorder in Robery Buchlyvie, the
self-made Scottish millionaire, are mild.
Even though he can no longer function
effectively because of his lust for power
and fear of death, he is saved by a traumatic experience. Medically, Buchlyvie's
recovery is quite possible.

Bridie gives another study of a victim
of a mental ailment in "Daphne Laureola"
(1949). Here, however, the symptoms
of a manic depressive are much more
advanced. The heroine of this play has
learned to attach so many wrong meanings
to so many of the situations she encount-
ers that her behaviour becomes grossly
inappropriate to the conditions that in-
duced it. The note of despair has increased and the atmosphere of "Daphne
Laureola" is dark indeed. The drama is
nihilistic. It shows us Lady Pitts, wife
of an aged British industrialist, who
cannot direct her activities to any major

purpose. She has alcoholic problems, a wide range of complexes, and is totally unstable emotionally. She is a modern liberated woman who has a hollow centre, having lost all traditional values. In this play, we get a glimpse of Bridie's Hell.

Now let us examine the plays more closely and see how the characters, especially Buchlyvie and Lady Pitts, develop the author's theme of the struggle between man and society. "The Last Trump" is one of those Bridie plays in which the author wrote like a good doctor and a mature dramatist. The play opens with a brisk and happy attention to the character of Buchlyvie, a financier whose love of good food and passion for good propositions have laid him, panting and furious, but not low, in a Glasgow nursing home. Attired in pyjamas and a dressing-gown of loud hue, his bed strewn with reports and blueprints, he operates the first moves in his new project, a hydro-electric scheme in a remote Scottish glen.

Invective levelled at those who would frustrate him sparkles around the head of his unmoved and efficient secretary. He is mortally afraid that even though he is only fifty, he is going to die. Buchlyvie is a greedy, irascible, ruthless man, whose life has been one long quest for more and yet more power. He has kinship with Lord Pascal and Mr. Burmeister of "The Switchback".

The high point dramatically of the first act is the battle of words between Buchlyvie, the scared materialist, and Sir Gregory Butt, a wise old physician. The specialist's examination of Buchlyvie and subsequent diagnosis provides an absorbing and tightly sprung satirical scene between the two men who worship such different gods. The contrast between them is dramatically intense; Buchlyvie pushing and ruthless but with the courage of his desires; and Sir Gregory, calm and expert, sparing of the word but unsparing in his professional interest, witty and devastating when roused – and the ill financier rouses him. Sir Gregory diagnoses angina pectoris and gives the patient a piece of his mind:

Butt: What you are now – a pitiable bladder of bloodshot lard – is the consequence of a life of gluttony and sloth.

Buchlyvie: Sloth! Do you know how many hours a day –

Butt: Aye. You think you're a mountain of energy. A fat sow in a field can muster enough nervous force to root for what it wants. Your only motive power is greed, sir, half a dozen different kinds of greed. [1]

The specialist goes on to tell Buchlyvie that his arterier are "like a mouldering heap of rusty drain-pipes." The rich businessman who has been getting heart palpitations, especially after he loses his temper, which is often, is really afraid of dying. He meekly agrees to Sir Gregory's suggestion to take things easy and rest in the country:

Do you know a place called Knocklarach? I've taken a house up there. I am interested in a company that's doing a bit of civil engineering in the neighbourhood. I am going up there to live. I am going to cut out drinking and smoking and live on the moors. I'll fish and shoot and give an eye to the business the odd time. Is that right?

The specialist realizes that Buchlyvie's good resolutions of a reformed life may not be enough to save him unless he also has a change of heart and controls his passions and conquers his fear of death. For he is still merely a terrified hypochondriac.

Sir Gregory is one of the best drawn of all Bridie's characters who belong to the medical profession. He is a man dedicated to the alleviating of pain and a doctor concerned with the spiritual well-being of his patients. He knows that Buchlyvie's mental state is much worse even than his physical condition, which is not good.

He also realizes Buchlyvie, in order to be saved, must be given a bigger fright than he can give him. He remarks to his associate, Dr. Griswood, that, if they could only sweep the small, murdering fear of death out of their patient, they could give him a new lease on life. This man's work and his personal fears are in partnership to accomplish his destruction. He concludes by saying:

> If we could convince this fellow that the earth would be hit by a planet within a week, he'd have the week of his life. But the Almighty isn't going to crucify the Universe for a rat like that.

Thus, the audience gets a skilful diagnosis of the mental ailment of the protagonist. Buchlyvie is a type of character that is familiar to the twentieth century, and his salvation is the main theme of the play.

After Sir Gregory departs, MacPhater,

the traditional 'keeper' of the glen that will be flooded by Buchlyvie's hydro-electric project, comes into the sick man's room by mistake. There is a battle of wits between the two in which again we see that Buchlyvie is an ill man. The MacPhater's land is heavily mort-gaged. The clan chief's financial em-barrassment has given rich Buchlyvie the advantage he needs. Buchlyvie is already in possession of most of the lonely glen Knocklarach. However, the bankrupt laird still holds a strategic hill on which a brilliant American astronomer, Dr. Schreiner, has installed a large telescope. Buchlyvie fails in his efforts to bully the Highland aristrocrat.

While MacPhater is putting Buchlyvie in his place, the audience knows what the two men know — that MacPhater's wife is dying in childbirth in the same nursing-home. This adds a delicate and deep pathos to the situation of the old clan chief and heightens the drama of the argument. Although Buchlyvie is con-temptuous of MacPhater's viewpoint, he does show some sympathy for the man himself. We have a glimpse of what kind of person Buchlyvie would be without his obsession.

In the next scene, the sub-plot domin-ates the action; it involves the struggle between Buchlyvie and his son, Tom. The Buchlyvie family, comprising the tycoon's dreary, snobbish wife, his religious crank of a sister Anna, his son Tom, who might be described as the decent, but drab side of his father, and Jean MacRae, Tom's fiancee, a girl of spirit whom Mrs. Buchlyvie resents, are all in an anti-room awaiting the specialist's verdict. It is clear from this scene that Buchlyvie is trying to hold Tom back from matrimony until the youth should have a measure of his own materialistic power, so Tom's fight for Jean is to ride with Buchlyvie's struggle with the Mac-Phater for mastery of the remote glen Knocklarach. The domestic squabble is less interesting than the scene in which Buchlyvie and Sir Gregory clash.

Act II finds Buchlyvie, his family, Dr. Griswood and the nurse ensconced in the castle which once belonged to the MacPhaters. Jean is there too, being fought for by Tom. He is still too much of a gentleman to accept Jean's offer of free love during the long wait they expect for parental approval of the match. But the sub-plot and domestic twittering of the ménage are soon silenced by the entrance of Professor Scheiner.

The astronomer breaks in on the Buchlivies late at night during a violent

rainstrom with the announcement that the
world will end in a few hours. The in-
mates of the castle do not know that
Schreiner, who has described Buchlyvie
as "a God-damned ruffian", is only playing a cruel practical joke on the greedy
tycoon. The well-known scientist con-
vinces Buchlyvie and his guests that the
earth will come to an end "when the sun
explodes at five minutes after five tomorrow morning". Jean is the only one
of the party who does not believe Schreiner's plausible theory. The scientist hopes
that the fear of the world's sudden end will
kill his enemy. He declares as he goes
out into the storm: "...sit and sweat.
You've five hours of mortal fear before
you, Buchlyvie; if the fear does not kill
you before the end, you rat".

Wise old Sir Gregory Butt is correct.
The crises brings out the best that is in
Buchlyvie. Far from dying of fear, he
takes a large drink and becomes most
philosophical about the brief future that
he expects to live. He declares that he
is no longer afraid: "There is nothing
any more to be afraid of".

The local Presbyterian Minister
suggests that they all go to the castle
chapel: "These places were built against
such an occasion as this." The very
reverend Dr. Craw is an ineffectual

minister of God. Like the churchman in "A Sleeping Clergyman", he does not represent a positive philosophy by which men can run their lives. Mrs. Buchlyvie informs the company that the chapel has been used as a tool-shed: "it is full of packing-cases and sacking and rubbish." Buchlyvie, who has never gone to church since his son was christened, agrees to help in clearing the chapel until he can think of something better to do before the last trumpet sounds.

The real character of the people in this play is brought to the fore by Schreiner's prediction of imminent doom. Buchlyvie and Jean MacRae come into their own while Dr. Griswood, Tom and Nurse Pettigrew are almost too stunned to think properly. The other members of the party retreat into the chapel to watch and pray for the coming of the end.

The final scene of the play begins with Buchlyvie, Jean, Griswood, Tom and the nurse playing poker. Jean, who has just learned how to play the card-game, is winning enormous sums of money from her host who is gaily philosophical about life in general. The actions of the tycoon prove the diagnosis of Sir Gregory. He is no longer obsessed either with the half dozen different kinds of cravings that have dominated his life for years, nor with the fear of death. Buchlyvie is much happier losing his money than he ever was making it. He is on top of the "disintegrating" world, and the captain of his soul.

The world does not come to a fiery end, but the tired card-players watch the dawn break over the lonely Grampians. The other members of the house-party, meanwhile, have fallen asleep during their night-long vigil in the chapel. The curtain falls with a kinder, more human Buchlyvie consenting to the marriage of his son with Jean, who is now a wealthy woman in her own right. The financier, who is completely recovered, is also discussing the commercial possibilities of the cosmic rays that Schreiner has discovered.

"The Times" critic, in reviewing the first performance of "The Last Trump", brings out Bridie's interest in the individual:

Every prophet with a vision of Judgement Day prophecies in terms of his own ruling passion. Anatole France maintained that the last utterance of mankind would be critics..... Mr. Wells, more interested in the wonders of science than in humanity, pictured mankind a rushing, whirling mass as the strange star from outer space grew larger, hotter, and brighter. Mr. Bridie judges the events in terms of character.[2]

Bridie does not always show his individual portraits with such care as he does in this drama. For example, Daphne Laureola depends more on herself than does Buchlyvie; some of the smaller parts of "Daphne Laureola" are carelessly written, but Buchlyvie is beautifully served. His change of character is credibly done if the audience accepts the dramatic device of 'Deus ex machina', involving Professor Schreiner. Buchlyvie is suffering from a mental disease at the commencement of the play, but by the final curtain he is cured.

One must examine this play as a whole. It has structural unity. "The Last Trump" has a plot and a sub-plot. They dovetail. The details of the play combine to build up the portrait of the protagonist that is the central point of interest in the play. This may be the reason that Bridie put Sir Gregory Butt, one of the most satisfactory characters he ever drew, into Act I and not into Act II. He gave us a complete portrait of Sir Gregory, a completion which simply made the act — the argument between Buchlyvie and the specialist. Bridie left out Sir Gregory in the last act because the specialist was present in the materialization of his psychological hypothesis, and what we lost by the absence of Sir Gregory's delightful company we gained by Buchlyvie's fascinating dance-of-never-mind-death to Sir Gregory's tune. If the specialist had appeared in Act II, he might have over-shadowed Buchlyvie who is the pivotal character of the play. Bridie's description of Sir Gregory calls for "a grey, wizened old man with gold spectacles and a heavy stoop." His delivery should fit that description, a rather dry, quiet, but clear, voice with an efficient snap to it: austerity and true authority parrying the bellowing, bombastic voice of Buchlyvie. There is skilful balance of characterization in this play.

It is interesting to point out that the mature Buchlyvie is well-adjusted and sees reality as it really is. He has grown in wisdom, and has thus controlled his selfish impulses. Like Dr. Mallaby in "The Switchback" and the schoolmaster in "Mr. Gillie", Buchlyvie has no delusions of grandeur. The traumatic experience he has undergone, makes him a more humble and understanding man. When it is realized that "The Last Trump" centres on Buchlyvie, the play has dramatic unity. And it fits into the pattern formed by Bridie's significant plays.

The other play for discussion in this chapter, "Daphne Laureola", was written two years before the author's death in 1951. It contains the most fascinating female character study to be found in all of Bridie's plays. The drama is one of loneliness, despondency, and gloom. Happiness and fulfilment can never come to Lady Katherine Pitts, the "Daphne Laureola" of the title. And so, in spite of all the technical excellences and praise-worthy qualities of the play, it must be called nihilistic. Lady Pitt's struggle with society dominates the action. Bridie's one full-length portrait of a woman proved to be his most popular London success. It was an immediate 'hit' and broke the record for advance bookings at the Wyndham Theatre. It ran for a year and the critics were delighted with the play. The dramatist has apparently caught the mood and atmosphere of post-war London with all its shortages, restrictions, regulations, and the austerity of its weed-covered, bombed-out ruins.

The play opens with Lady Pitts, who is the middle-aged wife of an elderly baronet, dining alone in a Soho restaurant. She drifts into dignified drunkenness and holds the attention of the other diners at "Le Toir Aux Porcs" with her intriguing, uninhibited comments. She doubts that Europeans can pick up the pieces and start a new life because of the war. She is full of hopeless despair:

It always happens. 'An hundred generations, the leaves of autumn, have dropped into the grave.' And again we shiver miserably in the confines of a long winter, as Christendom and the Roman Empire did hundreds of years ago. Again and again and again and again we have covered the face of the earth with order and loveliness and a little justice. But only the face of it. Deep down below the subterranean brutes have bided their time to shake down our churches and palaces and let loose the little rats to sport among the ruins. [3]

Here we see Bridie's protagonist perplexed by the enigma of human existence.

Greek mythology provides the source of this drama. [4] Daphne, according to the ancient legend, was the nymph who fled Apollo's embraces until her father, the river god, turned her into a laurel tree. Bridie makes that fugitive nymph become a twentieth century emancipated woman who is intellectually frustrated and sexually repressed. She appears to be a symbol of disillusioned innocence in Britain after the Second World War, and by extension, a symbol of general decay of western civilization. The working out of the play's symbolism is not entirely satisfactory. However, Lady Pitts' inability to face up to the cruel realities of life in post-war Britain is a problem that was wide-spread in the late 1940's. This play aptly catches the spirit of hopelessness and inner decay that was prevalent in the years immediately following the last war.

The mysterious woman of the title, who is introduced to us in a dingy bomb-gutted London restaurant, is in full evening dress, the elegance of which is in marked contrast to her surroundings and to her intoxicated monologue. Before a forceful and liveried chaffeur takes her away, a fiery young 'Displaced Person', Ernest Piaste, falls under the spell of her charm. This young Pole tries to prevent her departure, but ends up unconscious on the floor. On leaving, she asks all the diners in her vicinity to tea the following Sunday.

The seven ill-assorted patrons of the "Toir aux Porcs" duly appear at the residence of the rich industrialist, Sir Joseph Pitts, the next Sunday afternoon.

Lady Pitts, who is emotionally unstable and an alcoholic, has no recollection of what occurred in Soho, but accepts the entrance of her unknown guests with well-bred philosophy.

Ernest Piaste, whose father was Polish and mother was Presbyterian Scottish, and who is thinking of becoming an English non-conformist minister, is infatuated with his beautiful middle-aged hostess. His heart has cried 'Goddess' when he first encountered Lady Pitts in the restaurant, and he declares his love for her after getting rid of the other guests. Lady Pitts gently but firmly tries to explain to the romantic foreigner the difference between Lady Pitts in St John's Wood and Daphne under the influence of Bacchus in a run-down Soho eating house. The first suffers loneliness; the second exploits it:

Ernest:   It cannot be that the unique and exquisite can be anything but lonely.

Lady Pitts:   My loneliness finds expression only in drunkenness or in delirium. At other times I say: 'Keep off; keep far away from me.'

Such a statement would make the average

young Englishman with a passion for an older woman shrink in disgust, but Ernest is not an average young Englishman; he is a young Polish exile, solemn and serious, who is wrapped up in an unreal world created by his dreams. What he and Lady Pitts have in common is an eccentric form of loneliness. Not the same eccentricity, but it is as if two plants of different species have each produced in addition to the blooms natural to them one strange bud in common. For Lady Pitts it flowers in the moment when Ernest, ignoring her rational analysis of her anything but divine nature, makes his own hungry yearning companion to her own loneliness. But this impact is momentary, for Lady Pitts is a complex creature whose brilliant academic attainments in her youth achieved nothing more satisfying for her than a cage for her woman's instincts, the cage of the Modern Business Woman, and who, in middle age, was rescued by her marriage to Sir Joseph Pitts. The elderly millionaire, who has refined tastes, can afford to keep a rare specimen of the modern emancipated woman under glass. To Sir Joseph she is a collector's item, a unique laurel, a Daphne Laureola. While the young foreigner is giving Lady Pitts the passionate kiss, they are interrupted by the husband.

In Act III, a week later, Ernest, who is still enchanted and obsessed with Lady Pitts, is discovered hiding in the garden by the wise octagenarian, Sir Joseph, who listens understandingly to the young man explain why he is there. Then the elderly gentleman tells Ernest the story of his wife's life. He is too old and too philosophical to be jealous, or even annoyed with the young foreigner's passion for Katherine Pitts. She, the daughter of an English country parson, had won scholarships and first class honours in economics and modern languages at the university, yet could find work only as a governess. She was too intellectual to be happy at this so she married 'some kind of usher at a public school'.

Her husband was shortly afterwards killed in a mountain climbing accident, whereupon she obtained a position as secretary to a biscuit manufacturer in Birmingham, and ran a shelter for prostitutes at night. Sir Joseph rescued her from this existence by marrying her. He is fully aware of her drinking problem, of her loneliness amidst his wealth, and of her various complexes. Lady Pitts has suffered a nervous breakdown because she has been unable to come to terms with modern society. The understanding husband knows that s h e is always biting off more than the world and nature would let her handle. In Sir Joseph's words: "A woman can't carry all that and her physiology and psychology too". He also tells Ernest that the farther off she is w o r s h i p p e d the better, that soulful advances would only make her unhappier than she was.

Then t h e aged baronet ruminates on the causes of his wife's behaviour and on his marriage:

> In a way it's been a success and in a way it hasn't. She has outbreaks. One can't really be surprised. It's all this emancipation of woman. They can do what they like, but it's not in t h e i r nature to do what they like. T h e y just wallop about with the tide until they are caught in some n e w form of slavery. I found her plenty to do to keep her mind occupied, but there's more than the mind has to be kept occupied a n d so she h a s outbreaks every now and again.....I wouldn't mind her amusing herself with young men, but the trouble is she doesn't know how. She has the misfortune to be a dyed-in-the-wool Puritan.

Sir Joseph, like Sir Gregory in "The Last

Trump", attempts to look below the surface to find the root causes of men's actions. He feels that the psychological ailments of his beautiful wife, are due in part to the breakdown of modern ethical values. Modern social pressures have pushed Lady Pitts towards inner and insoluable conflicts. She was raised a Christian, but has since lost the faith of her childhood. However, she has not been able to replace it by any satisfactory code of ethics. She is a lost woman, who can no longer face up to the harsh realities of mid-twentieth century existence.

Ernest, who has listened attentively to the kind old Baronet, promises to worship Katherine Pitts from afar: "She will be to me as Beatrice was to Dante Aligheri, when she had gone to Heaven". He then becomes even more poetic and likens Katherine to Daphne:

For the laurel, Daphne, still eternally spreads her leaves, and the Sun-god, from ninetytwo million eight hundred and thirty thousand miles away, still warms and comforts her and endows her with life. It shall be so with me.

He then leaves Sir Joseph in the summer house, as the daylight begins to fade, and the chilly November day to wane.

Katherine finds her husband here a

few minutes later. The wise baronet
realizes that his wife is safe behind glass
like the Daphne Laureola bush beside him,
and that she is a collector's piece that
has to be sheltered and guarded from the
world. He tells her of his great love for
her, and falls back dead.

"The Catholic World" critic feels that
Sir Joseph's death becomes a scene of
unexpected emotion, and would have been
a triumphant last curtain.[5] It is true
that this is a powerful scene. However,
Bridie is primarily concerned in this play
in examining Lady Katherine Pitts. The
main function of Sir Joseph, no matter
how interesting he is in his own right,
is to throw light on the character of the
heroine. Lady Pitts is the focal point
of the play.

Nevertheless, the final act is dramatically anti-climatic. It takes place in
the same Soho restaurant where the play
began. It is six months later, after
Katherine has married her sinister
chauffeur-keeper, Vincent. By some
strange twist of fate, the same diners
as were there in the first act are gathered.
Although these minor characters are not
particularly well drawn, they supply the
down-to-earth quality needed to keep the
main action in proper focus. These reg-
ulars of the "Toit aux Porcs" are dis-

cussing Lady Pitts when Ernest enters.
When he hears that Sir Joseph is dead
and his goddess has remarried, he falls
down in a faint. He recovers as Katherine and her new husband enter the
restaurant. Ernest reproaches her with
his disillusionment and despair. She
has shattered his dream by marrying
Vincent.

She turns on him and accuses him of
trying to make a goddess out of someone
who is merely a poor, weak, lonely
mortal. Katherine's defiant speech is a
brilliantly flung truth. Speaking of Ernest's love for her which is inextricably
mixed with his egotism, she declares:

.....they're in love with themselves,
are they not? They care nothing for
us. Do they? They make up something out of their heads and borrow
our faces and our bodies to clothe it,
like washing off a line.....I told that
fellow I had played the harlot over
half of Europe. He believed me. It
wasn't true, but he believed me. And
he did not care.....He wouldn't have
noticed me at all if I hadn't got tight
and made a fool of myself. I burst
in on his meditations and he said
'Hello, here's a woman, she'll do
for Beatrice'.....It never occurred

> to him that I was a human being.
> They're all the same unless they're
> pigs.  And the pigs are at least honest
> with themselves and with us.....
> That's why I've settled down in a nice
> clean pig sty.

Katherine has no illusions about her new husband, but is willing to settle for second best.  She knows that Vincent loves her money more than he does her, but will let her continue to live in the hot-house that Sir Joseph had built. After advising Ernest to find something else to worship from afar, she leaves, and almost at once he has seized on another fancy. He realizes that he will never be able to break the fascination for Katherine,  even though he knows his goddess has clay feet.  Faced with his longing and loneliness, he cries:

> I am Apollo.  She is Daphne.  Apollo
> wanted Daphne so much that the old
> man changed her into a laurel tree.
> But Apollo still rode on his pre
> destined course, day and night, day
> and night.

The character of Ernest Piaste is well drawn and his romantic approach to life is in direct contrast to that of Katherine. The heroine of this play is bound by no illusions about herself or others. She fails in her struggle for identity. Katherine is anti-romantic and ironic, and regards most men as pigs. She realizes that Ernest's desire and love for her is 'calf-love', and that he is "an excitable, crazy, ignorant, young man, who is more in love with himself and his romantic dreams than with herself." She asserts that the young Pole is not so interested in her as a human being as he is in finding a visionary 'Beatrice'. She has been kept by Sir Joseph as an expensive rare addition to his collection of art objects for years. She knows that Ernest would have worshipped her and as well would have placed her on a pedestal. But Katherine rebels against this. She turns to Vincent, to whom she refers as "a faithful watch-dog, but a very stupid man".

By doing this, she loses her spirituality and joins the little rats sporting among the ruins. She can no longer cross over "the pit", but must walk around the hole in the middle of the diningroom floor. As a child she ate what she thought was the fruit of the tree of the knowledge of good and evil. The result has been that she has become too tolerant of the good and the evil she finds in herself and in others. However, she can only face up to this unintelligible, and at times almost

pointless human e x i s t e n c e  by getting
drunk every now and again. Her inability
to face up to reality and some of h e r
irrational actions, such as inviting every-
body in the Soho restaurant to her home,
are signs that Katherine is a manic-
depressive.

The portrait of Lady Katherine Pitts
is skilfully drawn. It would almost appear
as if her mental ailments were symptom-
atic of the age.  Bridie here stresses
man's isolation in an apparently meaningless universe. It is a play of profound
insight, of a broad and human poetic
quality expressed in the peculiarly sharp-
sighted vision of Bridie's most distinctive
work. There is no salvation for Katherine.
Here we have one of Bridie's non-conformists, one who has a distorted set of
values and is doomed to dwell in a twilight zone. Katherine can't adjust to
modern society. She has given up the
struggle.

In the two plays discussed in this
chapter, Bridie has made a clinical study
of some of the ills of his generation. He
realized that modern society causes
modern man to drift towards inner and
often insoluble conflicts. The individual,
while trying to remain 'true to self' may
break and cross the thin line into the
realm of insanity.

In "The Last Trump", Buchlyvie, whose symptoms of mental disorder were mild, is saved. But it takes his belief in an almost immediate total destruction of the earth to do it. However, Katherine Pitts, as we have already said, is beyond salvation. She has lost contact with reality; she has stopped seeing things as they really are, but regards them only in the light of her delusions. She is a pitiful figure - a lost soul. However, there is no evil in the sad heroine of "Daphne Laureola", who is likened to a rare plant. This cannot be said of the anti-social criminals who will be examined in the next chapter. To Bridie, the criminal is one who not only does himself harm by cutting himself off from society, but also turns on society and attempts to destroy it.

# CHAPTER V

## THE ANTI-SOCIAL PHYSICIANS

Throughout his life, James Bridie felt a fascination for the maladjusted members of society. We have seen in the last chapter how this interest resulted in Bridie's drawing characters of persons suffering from mental disorders in his plays. He was also intrigued by the amoral attitude of the criminal, especially doctors who committed murder. Bridie's murderers are characters whose actions, due to some form of mental ailment, harm not only themselves but the society which produced them.

Bridie wrote two plays dealing with anti-social physicians and murder. "The Anatomist" (1930) and "Dr. Angelus" (1947) are based on actual nineteenth century crimes that took place in Edinburgh. However, the playwright has taken liberties with the details of the events. Bridie is not concerned with giving us historical plays, but appears to be more interested in revealing the character of murderers on the stage. He

makes no final statement on the possible
causes of the actions of Dr. Robert Knox
in "The Anatomist" or of Dr. Angelus in
the play of that name. He merely shows
that uncontrolled individualism can have
terrible effects on both the person involved and on society.

It is worth noting that Bridie was not
interested in the sensational aspects of
the body-snatching scandal which shook
Edinburgh in 1832 when Burke and Hare
were tried for the killing of sixteen people,
and the famous lecturer in anatomy, Dr.
Knox, narrowly escaped imprisonment
for his suspected implication in the
affair. He was intrigued with the historical figure of Dr. Knox, and drew a
provocative, forceful portrait of the
British anatomist. Bridie's Dr. Knox
believed that he was a searcher after truth,
and that truth can be found in the accumulation of facts. To this lecturer in
anatomy at Surgoen Hal, the end - in
this case new scientific discoveries -
justifies the means - murder. Dr. Knox's
sense of values is completely distorted.

The focal point of the drama, which
has a macabre atmosphere, is the strutt-
ing, egotistical scientist whose powerful
personality dominates the piece even
when he is not on the stage. There is,
however, some ambiguity in Dr. Knox

because he is neither all villain, nor a martyr for scientific progress. The play draws its unusual strength and its subtle flavour of originality from the interplay of the contrasts which are revealed in the actions of Dr. Knox. His noble and humanitarian purpose is furthered by organized murder. Bridie does not concentrate on the two ghoulish grave-robbers, who turn to more direct methods of obtaining corpses when there are no new unguarded graves to supply the medical school with subjects for dissection, but focuses his attention on the strange anatomy professor himself.

In the opening scene of the play, we are given the portrait of a man of science who appears to symbolize the integrity of purpose of a great medical pioneer. Dr. Knox is a man above other men; he is a man dedicated to the progress of science. Science in his religion, and he needs no God. Dr. Knox explains his views thus:

Our friend Walter has a sacred thirst of which he is only half conscious. The vulgarian and the quack and the theologian are confronted with the universe. They at once begin to talk and talk. They have no curiosity They know all about it. They build a mean structure of foolish words and phrases, and they say to us, 'This is the world'.[1]

The anatomist maintains that he has curiosity. He institutes a divine search for facts. He is unconcerned with explanations and theories. He continues:

In time, when you and I are dead, his facts will be collected and their sum will be the truth. Truth that will show the noblest thing in creation, how to live. Truth that will shatter the idol Mumbo-jumbo, before which man daily debases his magnificence.

After his tirade, Mary Dishart, who is the fiancee of Knox's young assistant Walter Anderson, accuses him of using mere words. This charge is strongly denied by the anatomist:

Knox: It is a religion. It is a passion.

Mary: It is a very horrid sort of religion.

Knox: My dear young lady, it is less horrid than the religion of most of mankind. It has its martyrs, it has its heresy hunts, but its hands are clean of the blood of the innocent.

Mary: Do you call the hands of a resurrectionist clean,?

Knox: Of the blood of the innocent.

Mary: Grave-robbing is worse than
          murder.

Knox: Madam, with all due respect
          you are a pagan to say so. If
          you believed in an immortal
          soul, why should you venerate
          the empty shell it spurned in
          its upward flight, And with a
          false veneration too.    The
          anatomist alone has a true
          reverence for the human body.
          He loves it. He knows it.

This is Dr. Knox's position. He works
up the argument to a level where significant decisions are made, to the point
where all the characters in this scene are
showing their true colours. Knox himself
is vividly characterized throughout the
argument he controls, the argument on
which the rest of the play stands. It looks
as if we are to have the portrait of a
great medical pioneer. Here speaks no
rogue nor yet a man who will die for his
cause, but a man who will live for it,
ruthlessly if necessary, because the
cause is important enough.

On the other side, opposed to the
anatomist is Mary Dishart. She is un-
convinced by the rhetoric of Dr. Knox.
She is jealous of his hold on Walter and
sees the passionate dedication of master

and apprentice to dissection as immoral
fanaticism seeking to excuse, under the
heading of service to mankind, the vile
practice of body-snatching. She pleads
with her fiance to leave Knox, and accept
her uncle's offer of a good medical practice. Walter, very much in love, but
truly dedicated to the cause of scientific
progress, begs her to wait. Mary's
answer is a bitter tirade against dissection and Dr. Knox:

Mary: You come here reeking of
        mortality. It's disgusting.
Walter: It isn't disgusting. It's
        beautiful. Lovely, intricate
        human bodies. It teaches me
        to see God.

Mary: That's blasphemous.

Walter:No, no, no, Mary..... it's
        God's work. Anatomy is God's
        work. He made us and we
        ought to know how. It is as if
        they had taken the noblest of
        an artist's works and locked
        them up in a dark gallery and
        barricaded the door. We are
        breaking down the barricade.
        We"ll go on.....we'll make
        manifest God's work to man.
Mary: God's work! God and Dr.

Knox'. A singular assoc-
iation.....
Walter: Listen to me. Knox will be
remembered when Bonaparte
and Wellington are forgotten,
anatomy of the eye...

Mary is unmoved by either Knox or Walter
and breaks her engagement with the latter.
The first act takes place in the elegant
drawingroom of Mary and her sister
Amelia. The surrounding is in contrast
to the conversation concerning dissection
of human corpses. Amelia takes the part
of the distinguished visitor against Mary.
She enjoys the company of the forthright,
brilliant, if eccentric, Knox. She is
partly in love with him, but only partly.
She honours his scientific purpose, she
admits his importance. She understands
the man himself and finds something
essentially pitiful about this arrogant
bombastic lecturer who is the husband of
a woman of the vulgar class and who has
suffered a further loss of reputation
through rumours of his trafficking with
body-snatchers, but whose authority is
unassailable to his students and whose
delight in innocent and artistic pleasures
is bound up in herself. Knox has a naive
love of the flute. The first curtain falls

on this dandified lady's man, this cool receiver of bodies for dissection, playing the flute very badly. Here, we see another side of this complex character whose personality is pervasive.

The Second act opens with the unhappy Walter Anderson drowning his sorrow in a tavern which is frequented by the resurrectionists Burke and Hare. Walter is alone with the landlord until 'a glorious looking creature', Mary Paterson, enters with her rather scared friend Janet. The red-haired Mary, 'who has drink taken', strikes up a friendship with the befuddled anatomy assistant. The porter to Dr. Knox enters. When Burke and Hare arrive, it is plain from their sly conversation that the three of them have no scruples about the method used to procure specimens for the anatomist. A deal is made that the two Irishmen will obtain a subject for dissection for nine pounds sterling and the porter leaves the tavern. There is no suggestion that Dr. Knox has any part in the deal itself, but throughout the scene the power of his purpose penetrates. It is wrong to see the anatomist as a devil hovering over the grisly transaction. It is more correct to see him as a scientist who is perverted by being driven to depend on criminals for material that is vital.

The need for anatomical subjects was great for Edinburgh's famous medical schools during the early nineteenth century. The demand for corpses far exceeded the supply, and in the absence of official recognition of the anatomist's need, the whole thing became illegal, dangerous and disreputable. Knox has asked his porter to buy a 'subject' and prefers not to know how is was acquired. One of Walter's friends rescues the anatomist's assistant from the maudlin protection of Mary Paterson, and after they have gone, Burke and Hare serve drinks and blandishments to the befuddled young girl. The scene closes in on dialogue that projects a 'danse macabre' and ends with the two rogues assisting the drunken beauty out into the night to her undoubted doom.

Bridie informs us in the preface to the play, that the incident of Mary Paterson is taken from life. She was recognised 'on the table by William Ferguson, who later became the President of the Royal College of Surgeons of England. Fergusson is represented in the play by Walter Anderson, a fictitious character'. It must be emphasized that there is nothing in the character as written to make us pity Mary Paterson. She is a harlot of harsh voice and vulgar speech. She is

under the influence of alcohol w h e n she
comes on the stage and drunk w h e n she
goes off. The one gleam of pathos does
not appear until we can no longer see her
alive. The lock of red hair caught in the
lid of the c a s e delivered by B u r k e and
Hare early the next morning to Dr. Knox
reminds us sharply of youth and beauty
gone wrong. The part is all degradation
as Bridie has written it. In the stage
directions preceding her first entrance,
the dramatist says:

> Enter Mary Paterson and Janet. Mary
> a glorious looking creature. It is not
> apparent till she speaks that she has
> been drinking. She has a loud harsh
> v o i c e and her dialect is sometimes
> mincing and affected and sometimes
> pure Calton gutter-talk. The con-
> trast between her speech and her
> appearance is indescribable. Janet
> is a frightened colourless w i s p who
> has much earlier in t h e evening de-
> cided t h a t a joke can be carried too
> far.

This suggests that Bridie intended Mary
to be a wild, but not a really bad girl, who
is out on a spree. We can see from Janet
herslef that she would not associate with
prostitutes. However, Mary's character
is forged, not by stage directions but by

Dialogue, and a part must be finally evaluated by the words it utters. Bridie appears to be less concerned in the degree of harlotry than with the element of tragedy in the situation. The real tragedy of the tavern scene strikes the audience when a woman who looks like an angel behaves like a slut. The portrait of Mary Paterson, who is a social misfit, is well drawn. She snarls at Dr. Knox's porter, croons over the drunk, broken-hearted Walter, spits in the faces of Burke and Hare, then quietly goes off with the two murderers. Mary is pictured as a weak, wayward woman, but in no way deserving of her end on the marble slab in Dr. Knox's lecture hall.

The next scene opens with the hypocritical porter unctuously intoning the scriptures in Dr. Knox's rooms at dawn. A sobered, haggard Walter arrives moments before Burke and Hare with the promised body. He is completely unnerved when he discovers that the corpse is that of red-haired Mary Paterson. Walter commences to rave at the anatomy professor. The cool Dr. Knox then answers the hysteria of his young demonstrator:

Knox:  ...Murdered, eh? And suppose she were Dr. Anderson? Do you imagine her life was

so significant that we must
grieve at her death?  She looks
to me to be some common trull
of the streets...
You must not sentimentalize,
if you please, over my anatomy
room subjects.  You owe them
at least that respect...
It will be perhaps a satisfaction
to you to know that your friend
will be improving the minds of
the youth of the town in place
of corrupting their morals...
Come, my dear lad, I perceive
you have had a shock.  You
must not mind my rough tongue.
It is a defect in me as sentimentality is in you.  The life
of this poor wretch is ended.
It is surely a better thing that
her beauty of form should be
at the service of divine science
than at the service of any
drunken buck with a crown in
his pocket.  Our emotions,
Walter, are forever tugging at
our coat-tails lest at any time
we should look the truth in the
face.

Knox is in complete control of the situation.  His steely detachment almost
drives Walter distraught.  The assistant

attacks Knox, crying that he is a coward and a murderer. Knox easily handles Walter and sends him off to bed to recover from his hangover, saying he expects an apology in the afternoon.

The suggestion that the police be informed is dismissed by Knox in a grand manner:

Knox: You poroncephalic monstrosity. You will keep quiet, imbecile! You will gabble of nothing you have seen or heard or thought this morning. You will forget with that Lethe-like forgetfulness you apply to your studies. Do you understand?

Raby: I understand, sir.

Knox: Then go and help the janitor to prepare the subject. I shall demonstrate it to the class this afternoon.

In this scene we obtain a view of Dr. Knox different from that given when he was in the drawingroom with Edinburgh's polite society. The audience is forced to ask itself what is the cause of the unfeeling attitude of the anatomist toward the brutal murder of Mary Paterson. Is he merely a dedicated scientist? It is a question that Bridie must deal with in the

final act. Because he has lifted the entertainment value of the play into the sphere
of a dramatic thesis relating the attempt
of a medical pioneer to further a cause
that is human, as distinct from a crime
that has extenuating circumstances, the
answer cannot be in terms of villainy or
martyrdom, but must be of life which is,
in this case, something between the two.
In a sense, this is typical of Bridie. He
frames the question but never answers it.
T h e audience must draw its own conclusion.

After t h e dramatic intensity a n d
horror of act two, through which the
scientific detachment of Knox dominates
the action, we return to the cultural and
refined atmosphere of t h e Disharts'
drawingroom. Mary and Amelia Dishart
have just returned from a long continental
tour. The time is six months later, and
during their absence, the Burke and Hare
scandal has broken. Hare has turned
King's E v i d e n c e and Burke has been
hanged that morning for multiple murders.
The citizens of Edinburgh are outraged
at the authorities for not charging Dr.
Knox in connection with the case. The
mob threatened the anatomist with bodily
harm, but he remains cool and defiant.

Walter, who has recovered from the
m o o d of confusion that caused him to

accuse Knox of the responsibility for Mary Paterson's death, and the other students are still passionate supporters of their professor.

The final curtain falls on the imperious doctor lecturing eloquently and with enthusiasm on "The Heart of the Rhinoceros" in the elegant ladies' drawingroom. He appears to be talking about himself for his energy is sustained by no ordinary force:

> This mighty organ, gentlemen, weighs full twentyfive pounds, a fitting fountain-head for the tumultuous stream that surges through the arteries of that prodigious monster. Clad in proof, gentlemen, and terribly armed as to his snout, the rhinoceros buffets his way through the tangled verdure engirdling his tropical habitat. Such dreadful vigour, gentlemen, such ineluctable energy requires to be sustained by no ordinary force of nutrition.....

This is a dramatic and logical end for the play.

The author himself admits in a preface to "The Anatomist" that 'no solution to the mystery of Knox's attitude in 1828 is offered'. Perhaps Mary Dishart's sentiments in the third act are nearest the truth, though she only says it to hurt him.  She charges that the anatomist is 'a vain, hysterical, talented, stupid man'. She cries:

> I think that you are wickedly blind and careless when your mind is fixed on something. But all men are like that. There is nothing very uncommon about you, Dr. Knox.

This is, of course, not as Knox sees himself.  It is probable that he was not unmoved by the murder of Mary Paterson, but the moment of discovery demanded an authoritative and unemotional handling of the situation, to prevent his shaken assistants from losing their heads and giving way to their feelings.  This becomes clearer in his conversation with Amelia in the final act:

> Amelia:  .... I think of you galloping on a crusade with your eyes to the front, fixed on your goal.  How could you know that your horse's hoofs were trampling crushed human bodies.  You don't realize it yet.
>
> Knox:  Good God, Ma'am, do you think that of me! Do you think because I strut and rant and put on a bold face that my soul

isn't s i c k within me at the
horror of w h a t I have done?
What I have done ..... No,
I carry the death of these poor
wretches round my neck till
I die. And perhaps after that.
Perhaps after that..... But I
tell you this, that the cause
is between Robert Knox and
Almighty God. I shall answer
to no one else. As for the
world, I shall face it. I shall
play out the play till the final
curtain.

He compares himself to the great natur-
alist, Cuvier and believes that his work
in the a n a t o m y of the eye has already
made him immortal. This is a man who
is positive that he is a genius, and is in
some way above the laws of lesser men.
He must have anatomical subjects in
order to carry out his work. He maintains that the end justified the means.
Knox's confession to the effect that he
will carry the death of the Burke and
Hare victims round his neck until he dies,
is far more a courageous acceptance of
moral responsibility, than it is a confession of roguery.

Here, Bridie dramatizes the conflict
between human rights and medical pro-

gress. The dramatist, who was also a man of science, found himself moved to depict Dr. Knox as an egocentric genius. The anatomist deserves to be remembered for doggedly cutting a way for knowledge through the undergrowth of human ignorance in the teeth of suspicion and ostracism. But he must be condemned for the methods he used. [1]

The character of the anatomist, as we have noted, is ambigious. The ultimate truth about him is unknowable because Knox will answer to no one but Almighty God. However, only once do we get a glimpse of what may be the real man. This is when he is talking to Amelia, the woman he loves:

You understand me so well, so well. You see the little pink shivering boy crouching withinthis grotesque, this grisly shell of a body.

This play is a study of a doctor who is driven to become a criminal, or at any rate, to associate with murderers and grave-robbers in order to forward his scientific experiments. Bridie has been able to create an eerie, macabre atmosphere for his drama, with the brilliant if eccentric Dr. Knox being the character that dominates the action. The kind of individualism we see in Knox is that of a man who has convictions rooted in a twisted set of values.

Seventeen years after his success with "The Anatomist", Bridie returned to Scottish medical history to obtain background material for "Dr. Angelus". This play, as has been noted, is based on incidents involving Dr. Pritchard who was executed for poisoning his wife and her mother in 1833. But here the playwright up-dated the events, and set his drama in a Glasgow suburb in the post-war I period. However, Bridie has skilfully fused the two periods, so that the lingering remnants of Victorianism, as expressed in the setting itself and in the characters of the victims, produce an atmosphere in which an insane doctor of the twenties can operate with effective theatre.

Dr. Cyril Angelus, like Dr. Robert Knox in "The Anatomist", is one of the best characters that Bridie ever drew. He is a megalomaniac, who murders his wife and her mother because he feels that they are fettering his freedom. He is also a libertine, a charlatan, and an actor portraying a man of feeling, who suffers exquisitely the suffering of others. He almost gets away with his double murder.

In Angelus, we have violent contradictions. At one moment, he is merely a scullery hedonist, while the next he is a philosopher, a disciple of Sir Francis Bacon, and a wit. Then we see him as a cold-blooded murderer. Finally, after he is arrested by Inspector MacIvor, he breaks down, becoming a shivering coward. His brain appears to snap, and he is led away, declaring that his dead wife will return from heaven to speak on his behalf:

Margaret would tell you. She knows I was always good to her. Her blessed spirit is looking down from Heaven. Margaret! ....Help me! Come down from Heaven, Margaret. Bring some angels with you. They're going to murder an innocent man..... Margaret, speak up for me. You and your mother. Go to God and speak for me.....Oh, Jesus, tender shepherd, hear me, this cross is too heavy for me to bear, Margaret. [2]

The demented doctor has a magnetic quality about him, and his strong personality dominates his young assistant, Dr. George Johnson.

It is not that Johnson is a fool. However he is no match for the diabolically clever Angelus, who blackmails and flatters him into signing both the death certificates. At intervals, Johnson has qualms about Dr. Angelus, but he does not want to believe the truth. Johnson, an immature yet dedicated physician, is opposite to Dr. Angelus. He tells a patient that he feels his medical career is "like what the religious bloke calls a call. . . . . . It was a sort of holy quest, like the Holy Grail". He is blind to the faults of Angelus. Johnson cannot bring himself to accept his associate's guilt. He attempts to rationalize Angelus' behaviour and ignores the warnings of Mrs. Corcoran, a patient of his, as merely spiteful gossip against a fellow member of the medical profession.

Even when he becomes aware that Dr. Angelus is carrying on an affair with Jeannie, the sluttish maid servant, he justifies it in the same manner as he justifies himself when caught in a compromising position with the nymphomaniac Mrs. Corcoran - "After all, he is only human. There is often a side to the best of us we can't control".

Nevertheless, Dr. Johnson slowly and most unwillingly begins to suspect that there has been foul play in the death of Mrs. Taylor, and that Dr. Angelus is also poisoning his wife. His faith is shaken when he finds out that Angelus has collected a £10,000 insurance policy after the death of his mother-in-law.

However, the true character of the demented physician becomes clear to Johnson only after Mrs. Angelus dies. This second death opens his eyes to the faults of his idol. He is, however, physically prevented by the murderer from going to the police. Angelus is about to escape, when, alerted by Mrs. Corcoran, the police arrive.

Johnson continues to blame himself for not realizing sooner what Angelus was doing. He feels himself in some way responsible for the death of the two women. Inspector MacIvor reassures the young doctor that if the Procurator Fiscal and the Criminal Investigation Department of the City of Glasgow could not get off the mark quick enough to save Mrs. Angelus, "there's nobody going to blame you, and you little better than a bairn". The Inspector's final words to Johnson contain a mild warning:

> You young ones don't know the difference between good and evil. You should have a talk with the police now and again.

But MacIvor consoles him by adding: "You did your best and it was not very good and that's a fair epitaph for most of us". The trouble has been that Johnson was hypnotized by Angelus. Moreover,

Johnson was grateful at being made a full partner and he also was flattered by the older man's praise of his medical knowledge.

This play contains portraits of three physicians. They are well contrasted; Angelus is a middle-aged mountebank, Johnson is an earnest, gauche young man just out of medical school, while Sir Gregory Butt is an old specialist whose actions are dominated by a strong sense of survival.[3] Butt is called in to examine Mrs. Taylor. He realizes something is wrong about her death, but does not want to become involved with the case. He is an inhuman hypocrite. Johnson's character is too weak to stand up against the professional opinions expressed by Dr. Angelus and the medical specialist.

The protagonist in this play is completely egocentric. Dr. Angelus is dominated by delusions of grandeur. It is the devotion to self which has tyrannized Angelus. He has spent his life in running away when things have become difficult. He is the victim in part of his own too active imagination which results in his living in an eerie twilight world, in which, like Dr. Knox in "The Anatomist", he need obey no laws. He plays many parts from that of the old patriarchal master of the maid Jeannie, to that of the great

134

scientist who will some day make a major discovery. One minute, he is a pious Christian believer attempting to convert Johnson from his materialistic outlook and in the next a murderer, poisoning his wife.

We feel that Bridie has done a good job of depicting a man whose mind is deranged. Dr. Angelus is represented as a well-educated and widely travelled physician who commits murder in order to free himself from his women folk and from the drudgery of working. The selfish attitude of Angelus sharply contrasts with the selflessness and humanity of Dr. Mallaby and the teacher Gillie. In every respect, he is the opposite of Mallaby, who is a genuine medical researcher willing to contribute to man's betterment. Angelus, like Dr. Knox, wants the glory of making a scientific discovery. They both hope for immortality here on earth while Gillie obtains his reward in heaven. Dr. Angelus speaks in clich-ridden phrases. He suggests to his young partner that he cultivate the principle of a "moral holiday", for as he argues: "It strengthens one's moral constitution for the other days of the year. And it is very agreeable".

The dramatist has delineated for us the strange mind of an anti-social physic-

ian who explains his motives for slaying
his wife and her mother in this way:

Let us take a fantastic and laughable
instance. Let us suppose that he is a
doctor devoted to the study of his art
and determined to take his rightful
position as a benefactor to all mankind. He must have free play to the
wings of his imagination. He cannot
be cramped by the petty embargoes of
a general practitioner's environment.
Even the sanctions of his own earthly
animal nature tend to hold him fast to
the ground and they cannot be allowed
to do so. Suppose this man to have
made an unfortunate marriage. Suppose him to be subjected to the in-
cessant attempts of two ignorant and
narrow-minded women to mould him
into their miserable conception of
what a right-thinking domestic animal
ought to be. At every turn they trip
him with their beastly apron strings.
They are forever trying to lower him
into that barber's chair where Samson,
Judge of Israel, was shorn of his
strength. Suppose this man to have
passionate physical longings. Unless
they are satisfied he cannot plan, he
cannot think, he cannot invite his soul,
he cannot rise above the earth.

The protagonist believes that he is quite justified in liberating himself from the bondage of marriage by whatever means are available. He feels that he did right by murdering his wife:

> Margaret is at peace. Her weary journey is ended. She is in Abraham's bosom. And we can only hope that she's comfortable. Her story is told. To me, at least, it will always be an inspiration.

Cyril Angelus justifies everything that he does; he has gone on a permanent "moral holiday".

Here, Bridie gives us a terrible picture of a member of the medical profession who has lost all contact with the world as it really is. Dr. Angelus is an example of a person who carried nonconformity to frightening lengths. This play is written by one who knows every detail of a doctor's consulting room. It is authentic in setting.

The mental disintegration of Dr. Angelus, for all his philosophy, is complete by the end of the drama, when he is reduced through fear of the gallows to an hysterical, screaming animal. Angleus dedication to himself in his many roles has been total. He has declared:

The free spirit must rise and crush his would-be masters with as little compunction as if he were stepping on a disgusting beetle.

When he finally realizes that he is accountable to his fellow men for his actions here, he has a total mental breakdown.

The scene dominated by Angelus is contrasted with the one in which the police take over. A proper sense of proportion is emphasized by the matter-of-fact common sense approach to life's problems of Inspector MacIvor. He is not only a policeman who has both feet squarely on the ground, but he is also a symbol of law and order. The inspector leads us back into the everyday world after our glimpse of the nightmarish realm of the insane. Angelus has travelled further along the path of a megalomaniac than Knox travelled in "The Anatomist".

It is not surprising that this play caused quite a stir when it was first produced at the Phoenix Theatre, London, in 1947. Hunter Diack, the perceptive critic of "The Spectator", said:

There is a curious metaphysical quality about Mr. Bridie's new play. The illusion lies not in convincing us that the events before us are a projection of the real world, but in persuading us that the unreal world of Dr. Angelus' brain is for the time being worth more attention than any part of reality as we have known. Dr. Angelus, then, is 'of the theatre' in the fullest meaning of the phrase... Mr. Bridie's problem has often been to confine the rich flow of his ideas within the limits of the plot and character; but in Dr. Angelus he has created a mind easily capable of handling the flood of ideas and of retaining its peculiar integrity throughout all of the quick changes of mood... The mind of Dr. Angelus derives from that type of mania whose fears are forever ranging and whose moonstruck blethers are often sound sense peculiarly strung together. This is the mind which dominates the play and dominates it so thoroughly that we take sides with this larger lunacy against the callow, or moronic creatures who people the normal but lower world. [4]

The dilemma of modern man is seen in the subjective set of values that is held by Cyril Angelus. He at one time in his life must have merely been an eccentric. However, his eccentricity has gone beyond what medical science would call normal. He has passed over the line which divides the sane individual from the lunatic , and by so doing has become a failure. Yet, he cannot understand that he has done wrong in murdering his wife. He is beyond redemption. The weird world of Dr. Angelus shows the author in one of his most pessimistic moods.

It is doubtful if Bridie would have written plays as successful as these if he had not had his wide medical experience to call on. Bridie, the dramatist, owes a debt to Dr. O. H. Mavor, the famous Glasgow physician, who was his other self and whose rich medical experiences were invaluable. In "The Anatomist" and "Dr. Angelus", we see the dramatist's preoccupation with the individual's struggle with society focused on two members of the medical profession. Bridie recognised that genius is close to insanity and he had the greatest admiration for those forces and drives that are hidden within the human being.

We know very little about ourselves, and Bridie would be the first to acknowledge that science today still cannot answer some of the basic questions, such as "Who am I? " A study of his works would indicate that Bridie believed that non-conformity held within bounds was an admirable train in an individual. But when an individual ceases to see things as they really are, and when his set of values becomes distorted and twisted, as in the case of Dr. Knox and Dr. Angelus, he is mentally sick.

Finally, this dramatist was too intellectually honest to give his audiences easy solutions to the questions that men have been asking themselves since the dawn of history. He merely presents a medical case history, and leaves it to us to draw the conclusions.

# CHAPTER VI

## CONCLUSION

In the six plays examined in this thesis, James Bridie discusses the problems facing man in our strongly conformist society. It has been shown that Bridie's major concern and preoccupation was in portraying characters who rebel against society. By charting the protagonists in their several situations, it is hoped that this work has clarified and illustrated the predominant theme of conflict facing the individual in contemporary society. The dramatic unity of his plays arises from the fact that the problems he discusses have no resolution in themselves. The absence of resolution forms an integral part of the meaning of a Bridie play and is what actually culminates the thematic structure.

His dramatic patterns were not cut to accord with convention, but his dramatic themes were resolved in terms of his own logic. His characters and his handling of them, must yield, at least in part, the answer to the apparent riddle of this unusual dramatist's work.

We have limited our investigations to six plays dealing with the conflict between the individual and society. All these plays have a highly cultivated and sophisticated wit, and an intellectual restlessness that gives them considerable depth. Bridie displays a heightened awareness of the detrimental effects of social tensions facing the individual in modern society. Possibly because of his experiences as a physician, he always treats his protagonists, even though they are mentally unbalanced, in an understanding and sympathetic manner.

James Bridie is chiefly concerned with individual persons, suffering from a variety of psychological ailments and how they adjust to their environments. His interest in the nonconformist is seen in "The Switchback" and "Mr. Gillie". In these two plays, the difficulties of adjustment facing the heroes are not insurmountable. Dr. Mallaby in the former play and Gillie in the latter come to terms with their environment.

Bridie's work takes on a more sombre hue in the plays dealing with the mentally-ill. We are shown mentally disturbed protagonists in "The Last Trump" and "Daphne Laureola". The hero of the former play is able to recover because of a traumatic experience. However,

Lady Katherine Pitts in the latter drama, is doomed to live the rest of her life in a twilight world because of her inability to face up to reality. It is worth noting that the two World Wars, like other prolonged periods of united strain, left in their wake a wave of introspection and a return to the disoriented self-analysis that had been perforce submerged during the long years of group-action and group-thought. This may, in part, explain the great popularity of Bridie's plays, especially "Daphne Laureola".

While pondering on the question of right and wrong, Bridie's suspicion of the over-dedicated man is clearly seen in the works dealing with the anti-social physicians. In "The Anatomist", we have examined the all too familiar figure of a dedicated scientist who believes the end does justify the means. However, Dr. Robert Knox is not all bad. This cannot be said for the protagonist in "Dr. Angelus" who has gone on a permanent 'moral holiday'. He is trying to undermine the very foundation of society.

Thus, in the six plays examined in this work, Bridie demonstrates the results of three kinds of individualism. The altruism of Mallaby and Gillie are not recognised by their fellows. This has been the fate of other good men

# NOTES

Chapter 1

Note 1    This can be seen by examining his critical writings, such as
          A Small Stir, or Tedious and Brief

Note 2    James Bridie, Susannah and the Elders and Other Plays,
          London 1940 p. 78

Note 3    Tennessee Williams, Introduction, Camino Real, New York
          1944

Note 4    James Bridie, Tedious and Brief, London 1944 p. 18

Note 5    Ibid p. 15

Note 6    Ibid., p16

Note 7    J. B. Priestley, Introduction, James Bridie's Meeting at
          Night London, 1956, pp. VII-X

Note 8    James Bridie, One Way of Living, London 1939, p. 298.

Note 9    George Jean Nathan, The Theatre Book of the Year 1950-
          51. New York, 1951, p. 31

Note 10   Ibid., p. 32

Note 11   G. S. Fraser, The Modern Writer and his World, London
          1964, pp. 197-98

Note 12   Frederick Lumley, Trends in Twentieth Century Drama
          London, 1960, p. 223

Note 13   The Oxford Comparison to the Theatre, 1st edition Edited
          by Phyllis Martnoll, London 1957, p. 96.

Note 14   Eric Linklater, Art of Adventure, London 1948, p. 38.

Note 15   Ibid., p. 39

Note 16   Ibid.

Note 17   Moray McLaren, "Edinburgh Festival : Theatre,"
          The Spectator, CLXXXV, (August 25, 1950) p. 241

Note 18   A Sleeping Clergyman; The Amazing Evangelist;
          Holy Isle.

Note 19   For further evidence see Winifred Bannister,
          James Bridie and his Theatre, London 1955

Note 20   Peter Westland, Contemporary Literature, 1880-1950
          London, 1950, p. 257

Note 21   Ibid., p. 252.

Note 22   Allardyce Nicoll, British Drama, London, 1963, p. 310

Chapter 11
Note 1   James Bridie, One Way of Living. p. 41
Note 2   James Bridie, One Way of Living, p. 225
Note 3   Bannister, p. 24
Note 4   James Bridie, One Way of Living. p. 251
Note 5   Bradane was also a successful Glasgow physician who
         had turned to writing plays in the early 1920's. He
         was a founding director of the Scottish National
         Players, which produced his best play, The Glen is
         Mine in 1923
Note 6   James Bridie, One Way of Living, p. 278,
Note 7   Who's Who, 1950, London, p. 146
Note 8   James Bridie, John Knox, London, 1948, p. 72
Note 9   James Bridie, Preface, The Switchback, London,
         1930, p. 1.
Note 10  James Bridie, The Anatomist, London 1930, p. 20

Chapter 111
Note 1   James Bridie, The Switchback, London 1932.
         (All further quotations from this play are taken from
         this edition)
Note 2   Quoted by Bannister, p. 55
Note 3   James Bridie, Mr. Gillie, London, 1950, p. 74.
         (All further quotations from this play are taken from
         this edition)
Note 4   SPIV: One who lives by his wits --- within the law, for
         preference; One who earns his living by not working.
         Eric Partridge, A Dictionary of Slang and
         Unconventional English, London, 1961, p. 1289

Chapter IV
Note 1   James Bridie, The Last Trump, London 1938, p.13. (All further
quotations from this play are taken from this edition.)
Note 2   Quoted by Bannister, pp.140-141
Note 3   James Bridie, Daphne Laureola London, 1949, p.23. (All further
quotations from this play are taken from this edition)
Note 4   The use of myth as a basis for the play of contemporary life is
an important development of twentieth century literature. Bridie
uses Greek myth in this play as well as in The Queen's Comedy
Note 5   The Catholic World, xlvi (November, 1950 p.148

Chapter V
Note 1   James Bridie, The Anatomist, London 1961, p.20. (All further
quotations from this play are taken from this edition)
Note 1a  Winifred Bannister comments in a similar vein. See her
critical reviews of the play in 1930 and its London revival
in 1948.
Note 2   James Bridie, Dr. Angelus, London 1955, p. 80. (All
further quotations from this play are taken from this edition.)
Note 3   The character of Sir Gregory Butt in this play should not be
confused with the kindly and wise medical specialist of the
same name that appeared in The Last Trump.
Note 4   Hunter Diack, "Review of Dr. Angelus", The Spectator, CLX
(August 8, 1947), p. 173

148

# APPENDICES

## APPENDIX "A"

The place and date of the first productions of the most significant plays by James Bridie.

'The Sunlight Sonato' (or, 'To Meet the Seven Deadly Sins'). Glasgow, 1928.   (Written under the pseudonym of Mary Henderson).

'The Switchback'   Glasgow, 1929

'What It Is To Be Young'   Birmingham, 1929

'The Girl Who Did Not Want To Go To Kuala Lumpur' Glasgow, 1930

'The Anatomist'   Edinburgh, 1930

'Tobias and the Angel'   Cambridge, 1930

'The Dancing Bear'   Glasgow, 1931

'Jonah and the Whale'   London, 1932

'The Amazing Evangelist'   (one act) 1932

'The Pardoner's Tale'   (one act) 1932

'A Sleeping Clergyman'   Malvern Festival, England, 1933

'Marriage is No Joke'   Glasgow, 1934

'Colonel Wotherspoon'   Glasgow, 1934

'Mary Read'   (in collaboration with Claud Gurney). Manchester, 1934

'The Black Eye'   Glasgow, 1935

'Storm in a Teacup'   (adapted from the German play by Bruno Frank)   Edinburgh 1936

'Susannah and the Elders'   London, 1937

'The King of Nowhere'   Old Vic, London, 1938

'Babes in the Wood'   London, 1938

'The Last Trump'   Malvern Festival, England, 1938

'The Golden Legend of Shults'   Perth Drama Festival, Scotland, 1939

'What They Say'   Malvern Festival, England, 1939

'Holy Isle'   Glasgow, 1942

'The Dragon and the Dove'   Glasgow, 1942

'Mr. Bolfry'   London, 1943

"It Depends What You Mean'   London, 1944

'The Forrigan Reel'   ('A ballad opera')   Glasgow, 1944

'Lancelot'   Glasgow, 1945

'The Pyrate's Den'   Glasgow, 1946   (Written under the
    pseudonym of Archibald P. Kellock.)

'John Knox'   Edinburgh Festival, 1947

'Dr. Angelus'   Edinburgh, 1947

'Gog and Macgog'   London, 1949

'Daphne Laureola'   London, 1949

'The Tintock Cup'   (in collaboration with George Munro)
    Glasgow, 1949

'Mr. Gillie'   London, 1950

'The Queen's Comedy'   Edinburgh Festival, 1950

'The Baikie Charivari'   (or, 'The Seven Prophets')   Pro-
    duced posthumously at Glasgow Citizen's Theatre, 1952.

'Meeting at Night'   (after revision by Archibald Batty)
    Glasgow, 1954.

CHRONOLOGY OF THE LIFE OF JAMES BRIDIE
1888 - 1951

(This appendix contains facts concerning James Bridie and details concerning his forty plays that are not immediately relevant to the work).

1888 James Bridie, born January 3rd, in Glasgow, Scotland, the eldest son of Henry A. Mavor, a marine engineer, and Janet Osborne. His proper name was Osborne Henry Mavor.

1895 Mavor senior's financial position improved, and Bridie was transferred from the Glasgow High School to the Glasgow Academy 'for the sons of gentlemen'.

1904 Entered Glasgow University, and followed his father's wishes by becoming a medical student. Bridie did not have a distinguished academic career, taking double the normal time to obtain his degree. He read widely and wrote for the college journal.

1913 After remaining nine years at university, he received his medical degree and joined the staff of the Glasgow Royal Infirmary as a House Physician.

1914 On the outbreak of the First World War, Bridie joined the Royal Army Medical Corps. He served in the trenches of Northern France for two years before becoming ill.

1915 His father died of pernicious anaemia and overwork at fifty-six years of age.

1916 Bridie sent to the Middle East where he served for three years, mostly in Northern Persia and Russia.

1919 On his return from the war, Bridie bought a Glasgow practice, and commenced giving medical lectures at Glasgow's Anderson College.

1921 When he was appointed consulting physician at the Victoria Infirmary, Glasgow, he gave up his private practice.

1923 Bridie married Rosa Bremner of Glasgow. They had

two sons. The Bridies spent their whole married life in the Glasgow area, moving a total of ten times in twenty-eight years.

1926 Published his first prose work, "Some Talk of Alexander", which describes his life in the Middle East during the war. It was a commercial failure.

In the late 1920's, the busy physician became interested in the promotion of a Scottish national theatre. His friend, John Brandane, encouraged him to commence writing for the stage.

1928 Bridie was elected as a director of the Scottish National Players. This produced his first play, "The Sunlight Sonata", under the direction of Tyrone Guthrie. He used the pseudonym of 'Mary Henderson'. For the next decade, the successful Glasgow doctor led a double life as a prolific dramatist.

1929 Guthrie produced "The Switchback", which had been written several years previously and thrown into a drawer, in Glasgow, while Sir Barry Jackson directed "What It Is To Be Young" at the Birmingham Repertory Theatre.

1930 After a successful premiere in Edinburgh, in July, "The Anatomist" had a London run in October. He also wrote "The Girl Who Did Not Want To Go To Kuala Lumpur" for The Scottish National Players, and "Tobias and the Angel" which was first produced at the Cambridge Festival Theatre.

1931 The third play Bridie wrote for the Scottish National Players, "The Dancing Bear", had its premiere in the Lyric Theatre, Glasgow, in February.

1932 On December 12, the Westminster Theatre, London, presented Bridie's second play on a Biblical theme, "Jonah and the Whale". It was preceeded by his one-act play "The Amazing Evangelist". His only other significant playlet, "The Pardoner's Tale" (from Chaucer), was written at this time.

1933 Bridie's first play to be produced at the Malvern Drama Festival was "A Sleeping Clergyman", under the direction of Sir Barry Jackson. It had its premiere on July 29.

154

1934 Three of his plays had their premieres this year; "Marriage is No Joke" and "Colonel Wotherspoon" in Glasgow, and "Mary Read", which had been written with the collaboration of Claud Gurney, at Manchester.

1935 Only one play was written by Bridie this year, "The Black Eye"; it has its first performance in Glasgow. From this time, he was devoting more time to his literary work, and less to the practice of medicine.

1936 On January 26th, his free translation of Bruno Frank's German play, "Sturn in Wasserglass", had its premiere in Edinburgh under the title of "Storm in a Teacup".

1937 The London International Theatre Club produced his "Susannah and the Elders" in Sunday performances in November.

1938 Retired for the first time from practicing medicine, and celebrated it by writing three dramas in quick succession; "The Last Trump", which was first produced at the Malvern Drama Festival, "Babes in the Wood", which was presented at London's Embassy Theatre, and "The King of Nowhere", which had the honour of being one of the only modern plays to be performed at the Old Vic, on March 15th. Laurence Olivier acted the part of Vivaldi, the hero, in "The King of Nowhere".

1939 Bridie's 'Alma Mater', Glasgow University, honoured him for his contribution to both medicine and the theatre by bestowing an honorary Doctor of laws degree on him. His offering to the Perth Drama Festival, Scotland, was "The Golden Legend of Shults". In September, he rejoined the Royal Army Medical Corps, and served in it for the duration of the war in different parts of Britain. His autobiography, "One Way of Living", was published this year.

1940 After the retreat of the British army from Dunkirk, Bridie was one of the doctors that established emergency hospitals to receive the wounded in Southeast England. He also worked in London during the Blitz.

1942　On the request of the Pilgrim Players, a touring group of professional actors, he wrote two dramas; "Holy Isle" and "The Dragon and the Dove". Both had their premieres in Glasgow. One of his sons, a fighter pilot, was killed in action.

1943　The Westminster Theatre, London, presented his "Mr. Bolfry", one of his best plays dealing with the supernatural. At about this time, Bridie rewrote "Jonah and the Whale"; one version, "The Sign of the Prophet Jonah", was for a broadcast, and the other new version, "Jonah 3", called for only a small cast.

1944　In London, his "It Depends What You Mean" was produced, and in Glasgow "The Forrigan Reel" (a ballad opera) had its premiere.

1945　The Glasgow Citizen Theatre presented his colourful spectacular "Lancelot", based on the Arthurian legend. Bridie retired for the second time, and was made a governor of Glasgow's Victoria Infirmary where he had been a specialist for twenty-five years.

1946　The British government recognised his services in both the medical and literary fields by making him a C.B.E., while U.N.E.S.C.O. appointed him a director of its film section. His comedy, "The Pyrate's Den", which was written under the pseudonym of Archibald P. Kellock, was produced in Glasgow.

1947　James Bridie was one of the original promotors of the Edinburgh International Festival, and his historical play of overdedication, "John Knox", was his contribution to the first festival. "Dr. Angelus", after having its premiere in Edinburgh in June, had a long successful London run.

1948　Bridie was named chairman of the Glasgow Citizens' Theatre, which he had helped to found. His "Gog and Magog" was first produced in London.

1949　On March 23rd, the Wyndham Theatre, London, presented his "Daphne Laureola", under the direction of Sir Laurence Olivier. Later in the year, it was taken to New York where it was not well received by the critics. The only other play to appear on the

New York stage during the life of the dramatist was "A Sleeping Clergyman", and it also was a financial failure. His play written in collaboration with George Munro, "The Tintock Cup", appeared in Glasgow.

1950 Two of Bridie's most significant plays were produced in the last year of his life. "Mr. Gillie" had its premiere in Glasgow in February, and "The Queen's Comedy", referred to by its author as 'a Homeric Fragment', was his contribution to the 4th Edinburgh International Festival in August.

1951 James Bridie, after a brief illness, died on January 29th. He was in his sixty-fourth year. He was President of the Scottish Community Drama Association at the time of his death. His "The Baikie Charivari" was posthumously produced at the Glasgow Citizens' Theatre on October 6th, 1952, and his "Meeting at Night", after slight revision by his friend Archibald Batty, had its premiere in Glasgow in 1954.

# APPENDIX "C"

Characters of the six plays by James Bridie examined in this work, grouped under various headings.

|  | Protagonist | Physician | Clergyman | Successful Businessman | Dishonest | Mentally III | Eccentric | Criminal |
|---|---|---|---|---|---|---|---|---|
| SWITCHBACK | Mallaby | Sir Anthony Mallaby | ---- | Pascal Burmiest | Burmiester | | Aunt Dinah | |
| MR. GILLIE | Gillie | Dr. Watson | Rev. Gibb | (Kelly) | Tom Gibb Nelly Watson | | Gillie | |
| THE LAST TRUMP | Buchlyvie | Sir G. Griswood | Rev. Craw | Buch | Schreiner | Buch | | |
| DAPHNE LAUREOLA | Ernest | ---- | | Sir Joseph | Vincent | Lady Pitts | | |
| THE ANATOMIST | Knox | Watson | | | Paterson Burke Hare | | Miss Dishart | Knox? |
| DR. ANGELUS | Mr. Angelus | Dr. Johnson | | | Sir Gregory Butt | Angelus | | Angelus |

# SELECTED BIBLIOGRAPHY

## Primary Sources

Bridie, James    The Anatomist. London: Constable, 1961.
"    "    Daphne Laureola. London: Constable, 1949.
"    "    Dr. Angelus. London: Constable, 1949.
"    "    John Knox and other Plays. London: Constable, 1949.
"    "    The Last Trump. London: Constable, 1938.
"    "    Mr. Gillie. London: Constable, 1961.
"    "    One Way of Living. London: Constable, 1939.
"    "    Susannah and the Elders and other Plays. London: Constabls, 1940.
"    "    The Switchback. London: Constable, 1932.
"    "    Tedious and Brief. London: Constable, 1944.

## Secondary Sources

Bannister, Winifred, James Bridie and his Theatre, London: Rockliff, 1955.

Fraser, G.S. The Modern Writer and his World. Harmondsworth, Middlesex: Penguin, 1964.

Jeffrey, William. "James Bridie," The Oxford Companion to the Theatre. 2nd ed. London: Oxford Press, 1957.

Linklater, Eric. Art of Adventure, London: Constable, 1948.

Lumley, Frederick. Trends in Twentieth Century Literature. London: Rockliff, 1960.

Nathan, George Jean. Theatre Book of the Year 1950-1951. London: British Council, 1951.

Nicoll, Allardyce. British Drama. London: Harrap, 1963.

Partridge, Eric. A Dictionary of Slang and Unconventional English. London: Routledge, 1961.

Westland, Peter, Contemporary Literature. 1880-1950. London: English University Press, 1950.

Williams, Tennessee. "Introduction," Camino Real. New York: Mentor, 1944.

Who's Who 1950. London: Adam and Charles Black, 1951.

Catholic World. XLVI (November, 1950). 148.

Diack, Hunter. "Review of Dr. Angelus," The Spectator CLX (August 8, 1947), 173.

McLaren, Moray, "Edinburgh Festival: Theatre, : The Spectator CLXXXV (August 25, 1950), 241.

Priestley, J.B. "Introduction," to James Bridie, Meeting at Night. London: Constable, 1956.